T0162998

Death Where Is Your Sting?

This reflective book shows with generosity and openness how an Anglican priest in the present day, whose experience and vision has been informed by many years of pastoral commitment and care, might confront the reality of death on the basis of the accumulated theology and philosophy which we now find upon our bookshelves. Bob Reiss has organized his material carefully and thoroughly, and many readers will be grateful to find so many significant doors opened up to them. But this is more than a survey of arguments. The author's own search for an understanding that appears both realistic and faithful gives life and character to the whole book and yields a particular attraction and value.

Andrew Chandler, Professor of Modern History, University of Chichester

What happens to us when we die? Everyone has asked themselves that question. Bob Reiss offers us a wide-ranging account of different religious and philosophical perspectives, both historical and contemporary, on death. Whether you agree or not with his personal conclusions, you will find his book a truly fascinating and illuminating one.

Brian Pearce, Former Director of the Inter Faith Network for the UK

Spoiler alert: at the end of his book Bob Reiss writes: I therefore personally share Dag Hammarskjold' view 'For all that has been, Thanks! To all that shall be, Yes!' But I do not see any individualistic conscious life after death as part of what shall be.

Perhaps it is not really such a spoiler because unless you take the journey into the afterlife with Dr Reiss as your guide you will neither appreciate nor understand how rich is the material that has led him to his conclusion. One can only be thankful to him for providing such a pleasurable read on a topic which is, for many, so full of dread.

David Richardson AO OBE, formerly the Archbishop of Canterbury's Representative to the Holy See

Death Where Is Your Sting?

Dying and Death Examined

Death Where Is Your Sting?

Dying and Death Examined

Robert Reiss

CHRISTIAN ALTERNATIVE
BOOKS

Winchester, UK
Washington, USA

JOHN HUNT PUBLISHING

First published by Christian Alternative Books, 2021
Christian Alternative Books is an imprint of John Hunt Publishing Ltd.,
No. 3 East St., Alresford, Hampshire SO24 9EE, UK
office@jhpbooks.com
www.johnhuntpublishing.com
www.christian-alternative.com

For distributor details and how to order please visit the 'Ordering' section on our website.

Text copyright: Robert Reiss 2020

ISBN: 978 1 78904 247 4
978 1 78904 248 1 (ebook)
Library of Congress Control Number: 2020940132

A CIP catalogue record for this book is available from the British Library.

Design: Stuart Davies

UK: Printed and bound by CPI Group (UK) Ltd, Croydon, CR0 4YY
Printed in North America by CPI GPS partners

We operate a distinctive and ethical publishing philosophy in all areas of our business, from our global network of authors to production and worldwide distribution.

Contents

Preface   1

Introduction   3

Chapter 1. Ancient Beliefs and Philosophies   5

Chapter 2. Christianity prior to the Twentieth Century   31

Chapter 3. Jesus' Resurrection   48

Chapter 4. Modern Secular Developments   79

Chapter 5. Near Death Experiences and Neuroscience   112

Chapter 6. Christianity since 1900   132

Chapter 7. A Personal Statement   166

Postscript Facing Death   171

Index of Names and Topics   185

Books by Robert Reiss

The Testing of Vocation
Church House Publishing 2013
ISBN 978 0 7151 4332 2

Sceptical Christianity
Jessica Kingsley Publishers 2016
ISBN 978 1 78592 062

Preface

All sorts of factors lie behind the writing of any book, but among the ones that have affected me I must thank those who have read all or parts of this book and made constructive comments, all of which I have read if not necessarily agreed with. Will Baynes, Ralph Godsall, Clare Heath, Oliver Letwin, Brian Mountford, Brian Pearce, David Richardson, Jennifer Schwalbenberg and Richard Staughton have all assisted in that way and I am very grateful to them. While others might consider I am in all sorts of error, I know at least some others share some of those errors, although of course I accept full personal responsibility for what is said in this book.

I must also thank John Hunt Publishing, not simply for agreeing to publish this book, but for the very helpful way they have responded to my queries. As a publisher they ask a lot of the author in how the book is finally presented to them, but it has been well worth pursuing that course. The Endnotes at the end of each chapter contain details of all the books quoted in them, and I have not included an overall bibliography for the book as a whole. In the Endnotes for Chapter 6 I have included one other very recent book not directly quoted in that Chapter but highly relevant.

I must also thank my wife, Dixie, who has coped with my preoccupation with this book when no doubt she would have wished my mind had been elsewhere.

Introduction

Death and the process of dying are something that awaits us all. I am fortunately physically well, but as I am over 75 it seems a suitable time to think carefully about death and dying, and this book reflects my present conclusions. It is essentially a personal view and makes no claim to be a comprehensive review of the subject.

I spent my working life as a clergyman in the Church of England, retiring just over seven years ago from Westminster Abbey. Many may think that must determine what I believe on the subject of what happens at death, but in fact from the middle of the twentieth century there has been much debate about the subject, both in the Church of England and in the wider society; opinion even within the church is far more varied than many realize.

For me personally it was the death of my parents, my father over 30 years ago and my mother over 20 years ago that caused me to wonder about what I believed. Various friends, no doubt kindly, assured me that they were happy elsewhere but I could not help thinking at the time "How do you know?" That question has not left me and I referred to my doubts on the matter in my earlier book *Sceptical Christianity*. When the writing of this new book became a possibility, I was sure it was an issue worth pursuing.

Of course, some said that I couldn't know the answer, which at one level is obviously true, although probability pushes me very strongly in a skeptical direction for reasons I shall explain. Others thought it more important to pursue issues in this life rather than doubts about any possible future life. Yet I have discovered other people, including some in the church, have wondered about death, so trying to get my mind round the question seemed worthwhile, especially in a church where tacit assumptions seem to outweigh careful questioning reflection on the subject. Some asked "why disturb other people's faith?" That question underlies any theological reflection, but not to pursue serious questions because they might lead others to be disturbed can be no reason for ignoring the issues. Also, as I shall explain later, I have found my strong doubts about any form of personal consciousness beyond death far more liberating than depressing.

Chapter 1 examines what religions other than Christianity have believed on the matter in the past, and I have included in that some of the early Greek philosophers who were profoundly influential for many years after their own lives ended. Those who maintain all religions have consistently believed in life after death are simply historically wrong even though there have been long periods where some form of such belief was normal for some religions.

Chapter 2 looks at the development of Christian belief prior to the twentieth century and Chapter 3 examines the resurrection traditions about Jesus at the first Easter, including reference to three distinguished modern scholars who come to radically different conclusions.

Chapter 4 looks at some modern developments in more secular approaches to the subject, including – in some detail – four major publications written in the last fifty years that come to different conclusions.

Grounds for believing in any life after death are mainly either philosophical or religious ones, but there are those who have been brought to that belief as a result of personal experiences, particularly of what are known as Near Death Experiences and there is plenty of literature approaching the question from that perspective. That and the challenge brought about by neuroscience I examine in Chapter 5.

Chapter 6 examines Christian thought from the beginning of the twentieth century, where the debate has been more varied than many might imagine. That chapter covers the questions that have been most influential in helping me come to my own conclusions.

Chapter 7 provides an overview of my conclusions and the implications of them.

A Postscript looks at a related but different issue, that of facing the process of dying. In various parts of the world, not least of all in the United Kingdom, there has been much discussion on whether there are circumstances when those who request assisted dying might be granted their request. This is a profoundly serious moral issue that is not going to go away, and I have been pleased to be part of a small group, mainly but not exclusively of clergy who meet under the chairmanship of a rabbi to consider it. Over a number of years we have listened to some who have been personally involved in responding to specific cases and that has certainly affected my thinking. As a result I have come to disagree with the public stance of the majority of the House of Bishops on the matter and explain why.

Chapter 1

Ancient Beliefs and Philosophies

Until fairly recently religions have had a significant influence on what many people believed about death. This chapter considers what some non-Christian religions have believed about it and examines some of the ancient philosophical arguments on the subject.

What anybody means by life after death can be very varied. I suspect few would dispute one view, which is that when we die others will retain their memories of us. How long those memories last might depend on all sorts of factors, but except for those who become famous it is unlikely to last much more than 80 or so years after their death. I never knew my great grandparents and know very little about them; I suspect I am typical in that. But the memories of us will continue for a period, at the very least in the thoughts of our families, as was expressed in the book Ecclesiasticus in the Apocrypha "Their bodies were buried in peace, and their name lives to all generations"(44.14). However, such memories can change even after the death of the person concerned. Fame certainly came to some people after their death; Van Gogh, Kafka, Galileo and Mendel are all examples, but infamy can come as well; look at the memory of Jimmy Savile, who was given generally positive obituaries when he died until the details of his pedophilia became publicly known after his death. Other people's assessment and memory of us can vary for good or ill even after our deaths, so at the very least life after death has some meaning in such a context.

Others might dwell on the undoubtedly mysterious nature of consciousness. We all have a consciousness of self that is peculiar to us, but we also share a good deal with other people and in so far as in our lives we contribute to other people's consciousness that diffused consciousness also continues after our death. It may or may not be associated with the memories others have of us, but the fact that someone forgot from whom they got a particular idea does not stop it still being a part of their consciousness and even part of a continuing collective consciousness.

Other concepts are more definite about some sort of personal existence after death; they might include reincarnation, that when someone dies their "soul" passes on to an unborn child or even, in some views, to other non-human living creatures, or it might involve the notion of the immortality of the soul, that there is something about the human "soul" that survives death, or it may involve resurrection, that in some way our bodies are resurrected so that others will still know and even recognize us. There has also been the advent of the rather questionable activity of Cryonics, where a person's body can be frozen and kept in cold storage in the hope that scientific advances may allow them to be revived in the future, exactly how the brain would survive such an experience and then come back to life in a much-changed world is not at all clear. Interestingly, Yuval Hariri sees death as "a technical problem that we can and should solve."[1] He does, however, acknowledge that "the hopes of eternal youth in the twenty-first century are premature, and whoever takes them too seriously is in for a bitter disappointment."[2] More modestly, he hopes it might be possible over the next 100 years to double life expectancy to 150. Few of us will be around to see if he is right!

All of those views and variations on them – except Cryonics – can be found in the world's religions, although it is not correct to say that all religions believe in life after death.

Judaism

For much of the Old Testament the Jewish people were at the very least ambiguous about any afterlife. While they said that the dead went to Sheol, or the place of the departed, they were more concerned with the fate of the family and the whole people of Israel rather than with the fate of any individuals after death. There were exceptions; Genesis speaks of Enoch walking "with God; and he was not, for God took him" (Gen. 5.24). Moses' commissioning of his successor, Joshua, is followed by the story of Moses going up Mount Nebo, viewing the Promised Land and then in the last chapter of Deuteronomy it simply records "Moses the servant of the Lord died there in the land of Moab, according to the word of the Lord, and he buried him in the valley in the land of Moab opposite Beth-peor; but no man knows the place of his burial to this day" (Deut 34. V 5–6). There is also the strange story of Elijah being taken up into heaven by a whirlwind (II Kings 2. 11) and Saul's encounter with the dead Samuel through the medium of Endor (1 Samuel. 28; 7–25). But more often the Old Testament speaks of individuals like King David "sleeping with their fathers."

There was disagreement about what that entailed. Ecclesiastes, dating from the third century BCE, recognized that human beings and animals shared one thing: "For the fate of the sons of men and the fate of beasts is the same; as one dies, so dies the other. They all have the same breath, and man has no advantage over the beasts; for all is vanity. All go to one place; all are from the dust, and all turn to dust again" (Eccles. 3: 19–20). Later, the author summarized his view of human beings: "For the living know that they will die, but the dead know nothing, and they have no more reward; but the memory of them is lost. Their love and their hate, and their envy have already perished, and they have no more for ever any share in all that is done under the sun… Whatever your hand finds to do, do it with all your might; for there is no work or thought or knowledge or wisdom in Sheol, to which you are going" (Eccles. 9; 5–6, 10). Whether being in Sheol could even constitute existence is doubtful.

However, there are intimations of belief in an afterlife in some of the later books of the Old Testament, particularly the Book of Daniel, which appears to have been redacted no earlier

7

than the second century BCE, and those views were most clearly expressed in the later Wisdom of Solomon from the Apocrypha, written in the first century BCE. "The souls of the righteous are in the hand of God, and no torment will ever touch them. In the sight of the foolish they seem to have died, and their departure was thought to be a disaster, and their going from us to be their destruction; but they are at peace. For though in the sight of others they were punished, their hope is full of immortality" (Wisdom 3. 1–4).

Two critical factors seem to have brought about this change after most of the Old Testament was written. The Maccabean Revolt in the second century BCE against the Seleucid Empire, when many young Jewish men died at the hands of their oppressors, produced a motive for the development of belief in life after death; justice demanded those who had given their lives for Israel should be rewarded. The notion that the injustices of the world required some other world where they could be put right remains a significant factor in arguments for life after death.

The second factor was the growing influence of Platonism's belief in life after death. This was a surprising combination because the Maccabean Revolt was also against the growing Hellenization demanded by the Seleucid Empire; nonetheless Platonism's influence affected some Jewish thinkers, including the author of the Wisdom of Solomon, which was written in Greek. Platonism's influence also certainly imbued the early Christian Church as well, especially through St Augustine.

By the time of the New Testament those Jews who believed in the authority of the Written Tradition of the Torah such as the Sadducees, who were the guardians of the Temple in Jerusalem and who provided the High Priest of Jewish religion until the sack of Jerusalem in 70 CE, definitely rejected any notion of life after death, as was confirmed in the questions asked by them of Jesus in Mark 12. 18–27. However, such rejection was not universal. The Pharisees, who became a Jewish movement in the second century BCE after the war against the Seleucid Empire, followed the tradition of the Oral Law and believed in an afterlife. Géza Vermes, the Jewish biblical scholar, suggests that the answer attributed to Jesus in his conflict with the Sadducees in the passage in Mark was typical of Pharisaic arguments.[3]

After the fall of Jerusalem and the destruction of the Temple in 70 CE the Sadducees lost their purpose and the movement became extinct, hence Pharisaic Judaism became the predominant influence in the dispersed Jewish people. Thereafter there was a move to accepting the notion of life after death. Maimonides (1135–1204), one of the greatest Jewish philosophers of the medieval period, produced a commentary on the Mishnah that is still considered an authoritative codification of the Jewish law. It included his 13 principles of Jewish Faith, and belief in the resurrection of the dead was the last principle.

Today the picture in Judaism is more complicated. Orthodox Judaism is distinguished from Progressive Judaism, and Orthodox Judaism still holds to a notion of the immortality of the soul or of resurrection. Within Progressive Judaism there is both Reform and Liberal Judaism. Judaism distinguishes between *halakhah*, or legal norms of behavior, and *aggadah*, which includes matters of belief. In Progressive Judaism there is no single normative view about *aggadah*, but a wide range of opinion is accepted. Beliefs about life after death, which do not affect legal behavior, come within the area of *aggadah*. Progressive Judaism has also become more uncertain. Rabbi Mark Solomon from the more progressive liberal wing suggests that in that tradition the notion of an afterlife has almost completely collapsed. "The reconstruction of Judaism in the period of Enlightenment and Emancipation, in which huge effort was expended, from Moses Mendelssohn onwards, in portraying Judaism as an enlightened, rational religion of divinely revealed ethical laws, emphasizing righteousness for its own sake, downplayed the supernatural, miraculous and eschatological. Jews, reveling in their newfound emancipation, were at the forefront of movements of rationalism and cultural criticism. There was a strong desire both to make Judaism palatable, and hence tolerable, to liberal Christians, and at the same time to differentiate Judaism from Christianity.... There was a strong tradition amongst Christians that Judaism was a 'this worldly' religion, in a negative sense – materialistic rather than spiritual – bolstered by the fact that the Hebrew Bible barely speaks about the afterlife. As knowledge of rabbinic learning declined amongst assimilated Jews, I think it's possible that they absorbed this Christian (mis)perception and made a virtue of it.... The continued rise of scientific rationalism amongst western professional elites, among whom Jews were and are prominent, led to increasing skepticism about the existence of an immaterial soul and hence about an afterlife."[4]

He also believes two other factors had their effect. First, the Holocaust with the perceived failure of God to intervene and protect his people made belief in an afterlife a sort of disgraceful cop-out. It was this world that Jews thought needed fixing, not clinging to the cheap comfort of seeing your murdered parents and relatives again in heaven. Secondly, there was Zionism. Whether secular or religious, if one's faith and effort is invested in saving the Jewish people by creating a Jewish state, the focus is all (subconsciously) on bringing salvation now, on earth, and belief in heaven is just a distraction.

However, another Rabbi[5] also from the Progressive tradition but more at the Reform end of the Liberal/Reform spectrum tells me that in Reform Judaism the picture is more complex still, in that while many Reform Jews do not believe in life after death many are more uncertain. That is illustrated by a fascinating statistic. Orthodox Judaism follows the requirement of Deuteronomy that a dead person should be buried and not cremated, and it appears that for the Orthodox that partly flows from their belief in a final resurrection for all at the end of time.

In the UK population as a whole just over 75% of funerals are cremations, but in the Reform synagogue where Rabbi Freeman ministers, the figure is closer to 16%. That may simply reflect a desire to follow Jewish tradition at that point, but it seems also to show that within contemporary Judaism as a whole there remains a variety of opinion on the possibility of life after death.

The Ancient Greeks

It was the Ancient Greek Philosophers who probably gave most impetus to belief in life after death. "Pythagoras, often venerated as the first of the philosophers, was also renowned as a champion of survival after death. He did not, however, believe that at death the soul entered a different and shadowy world: he believed that it returned to the world we all live in, but it did so as the soul of a different body."[6] He believed souls transmigrated not just between humans, but across species. He "did not offer philosophical arguments for survival and transmigration; instead he claimed to prove it in his own case by identifying his belongings in a previous incarnation. He was thus the first of a long line of philosophers to take memory as a criterion of personal identity."[7]

Exactly what Socrates thought about life after death is not clear. Xenophon and Plato both give descriptions of the speeches in defense of Socrates at his trial but none of them can be relied upon as being historically accurate. Anthony Kenny compares the different impressions of Socrates given by Xenophon and Plato to the contrasting pictures of Jesus in Mark's Gospel and in St John's. "While in Mark Jesus speaks in parables, brief aphorisms, and pointed responses to questions, the Jesus of the fourth gospel delivers extensive discourses that resonate at several levels. There is a similar contrast between Xenophon's Socrates, who questions, argues, and exhorts in a workmanlike manner, and the Socrates of Plato's *Republic*, who delivers profound metaphysical lectures in a style of layered literary artifice. Just as it was John's presentation of Jesus that had the greatest impact on later theological development, so it is the Socrates of Plato whose ideas proved fertile in the history of philosophy."[8] "In Plato's *Apology* Socrates appears to be agnostic about the possibility of an afterlife... The Platonic Socrates in the *Phaedo*, however, is the most articulate protagonist of the thesis that the soul not only survives death, but is better off after death."[9]

The argument Plato puts into the mouth of Socrates in *Phaedo*, which is a dialogue between Socrates and some friends as he prepares to take the hemlock and die, is worth examining as it, or variations on it, were so influential later. He suggests that death "is nothing but the separation of the soul from the body. And being dead is this: the body's having come to be apart, separated from the soul, alone by itself, and the soul being apart, alone by itself, separated from the body."[10] He envisages the soul being imprisoned by the body and says "because the body affords us countless distractions... if we know nothing purely in the body's company, then one of two things must be true: either knowledge is nowhere to be gained, or else it is for the dead; since then, but no sooner, will the soul be alone apart from the body."[11] In response to his interlocutors' questions and comments Plato gives three arguments for the immortal nature of the soul. The first is often called the Cyclical argument and is about opposites, where it is suggested that in any set of opposites each comes from the other and needs the other, sleep and wakefulness for example, bigger and smaller, or death and life. As death comes from life so, Plato argues, life must come from death. On that basis it leads to the second so-called Recollection argument; knowledge is recollection, and recollection requires pre-existence, so he argues for the existence of a non-embodied soul before life as well as after death. Such a soul is immortal in the way for Plato ideas are immortal in his Theory of Ideas, illustrated by what he says about the notion of a circle. The Idea of a Circle is greater than any specific example of a circle, and it is not a physical thing, but belongs to a non-physical spiritual realm, which is more real than the material world or world of change. The third so-called Affinity argument, flows from the same idea, that unlike the body, which can disintegrate at death, the unchanging ideas with which the soul is concerned are indissoluble and continue after death; insofar as the soul has considered and adopted them it too will be immortal.

Each of those three arguments has been subjected to much criticism. David Gallop in his commentary on *Phaedo* says "Things come to be alive when they come into being at birth or conception. But from a thing's coming to be alive in this sense, the proper inference is not that it was previously dead, but that it did not exist previously at all. The sense of 'come to be alive' required for the argument is not that in which a living thing comes into being, but that in which a soul 'becomes incarnate' in a living body. Yet it cannot do this unless it already exists before birth or conception. And whether it does so or not is just what is at issue."[12] Anthony Kenny comments on the Cyclical argument "Is it true that opposites always come from opposites? And even when opposites do come from opposites, must the cycle continue forever? Even if sleeping has to follow waking, may not one last waking be followed... by everlasting sleep? And however sure it might be that the soul cannot abide death, why must it retire elsewhere when the body dies, rather than perish like the melted snow?"[13] That, and indeed even the very notion of "the soul," has been subject to much examination, as will be seen later.

However, even Plato was prepared to hedge his bets. In his Apology on the subject of death he put into the mouth of Socrates:

Let us also think in this way how great a hope there is that it is good: For being dead is either of two things. Either it is such as to be nothing and the dead man has no perception of anything, or else, in accordance with the things that are said, it happens to be a certain change and migration of the soul from the place here to another place. And if there is no perception, but it is like a sleep in which the sleeper has no dream, death would be a marvelous gain. For I would suppose that if someone had to select the night in which he slept so soundly that he did not even dream, and had to contrast the other nights and days of his own life with that night, and then had to say on consideration how many days and nights of his own life he had spent better and more pleasantly than that night, I would suppose, not that some private man, but that the Great King himself would find that they are easy to count compared with the other days and nights. If, then, death is such a thing, I at least say it is a gain. For all time appears nothing more than one night.... But now it is time to go away, I to die you to live. Which of us goes to a better thing is unclear to everyone except to the god.[14]

Aristotle held to a slightly different view of the soul. His notion was greater than simply something that human beings have, for he believed "The soul's very essence is defined by its relationship to an organic structure. Not only humans but also beasts and plants have souls – not second-hand souls, transmigrants paying the penalty of earlier misdeeds, but intrinsic principles of animal and vegetable life. A soul, Aristotle says, is the 'actuality of a body that has life', where life means the capacity for self-sustenance, growth and decay."[15] To that extent he was not a dualist: "it is quite clear that the soul is not separable from the body."[16] However, he thought the soul might have different parts, the desire for nutrition, for example, or the ability to move, but for human beings it includes the rational part. What was unusual about humans in distinction from animals is that there was within the human soul a process of rational thought so that the desires that were part of the soul could be constrained by the capacity of rational thought. He wrote "It remains unclear whether the soul is the actuality of a body in this way or rather is as the sailor of a boat."[17] Although his teaching was not clear on the matter it seemed that he did believe that a purely rational element might in some way survive death. Through St Augustine, Plato's influence on Christianity was far greater than Aristotle's until St Thomas Aquinas found a way of combining Aristotelian philosophy with his understanding of Christian faith, as Maimonides did with the Jewish faith. The notion that each human being had a soul that was independent of the body had a profound effect on early Christian and later medieval views of life after death.

However, not all early Greek philosophers believed in it. One of Socrates's friends in *Phaedo*, Cebes, says to him "what you say about the soul is the subject of much disbelief: men fear that when it has been separated from the body, it may not exist anywhere, but that on the very day a man dies, it may be destroyed and perish, as soon as it is separated from the body."[18] Epicurus, who lived after both Plato and Aristotle, believed that the death of the body was also the death of the soul. He wrote to Menoeceus "Death does not concern us, because as long as we live death is not here. And once it comes, we no longer exist."[19] He wanted to remove the fear of death, which he thought was generated primarily by religion as it held out the prospect of suffering after death, which Epicurus considered to be an illusion. Seneca was a Stoic philosopher at the beginning of the Christian era; he was born in 4 BCE and died in 65 BCE. He wrote extensively on the subject of death, perhaps inevitably for someone living through the reigns of Caligula and Nero, the latter ordering Seneca's death. His views on life after death are not clear, sometimes he seemed to accept Plato's theme of immortality, but more often he was concerned to assert that no one should be afraid of death.

Consider that the dead are afflicted by no ills, and that those things that render the underworld a source of terror are mere fables. No shadows loom over the dead, nor prisons, nor rivers blazing with fire, nor the waters of oblivion; there are no trials, no defendants, no tyrants reigning a second time in that place of unchained freedom. The poets have devised these things for sport, and have troubled minds with empty terrors. Death is the undoing of all our sorrows, an end beyond which our ills cannot go; it returns us to that peace in which we reposed before we were born. If someone pities the dead, let him also pity those not yet born.[20]

The influence of ancient Greek philosophers ranged across a whole series of matters including death, although for Christianity at least, especially through St Augustine, Plato won the day until Aristotle replaced him via St Thomas Aquinas.

Islam

Islamic belief is centered on the Qur'an, which Muslims hold to be the accurate word of God as dictated to Muhammad. His faithful followers have no doubt that that the Qur'an came directly from God via the angel Gabriel and takes precedence over any other area of human knowledge. The Qur'an itself speaks of a Day of Resurrection and of a final Judgment, so for a Muslim they are indisputable.

The Qur'an gives a high status to both Moses and Jesus, although it denies that Jesus died on the Cross but rather asserts that he was taken directly into heaven. Also in Islam there is no sense that one person's sacrifice can affect another person's final judgment. On the Day of Judgment, the deeds of each person will receive their exact reward and while repentance before death might be met by the mercy of God after death there is no room for repentance.

Central to Islam is the notion of the soul, with some recent discussions suggesting that "ensoulment" happens at the end of the first four months of pregnancy.[21] An overall description of Islamic belief from an Islamic scholar, Dr Usama Husan, states:

Muslim belief is that human souls are on a journey that is much greater than earthly lifespans. All souls began in the knowledge of God, and they were all asked, 'Am I not your Lord?' To this they all replied, 'Yes'.[22] These souls eventually join with bodies in the material world. The 'life of this world' is temporary. 'Every soul tastes death'[23] as the Qur'an proclaims, and then moves into a state that is the beginning of the Hereafter (after life), but the precursor to the final judgment on the Day of Resurrection. A popular belief is that after judgment, all souls eventually live forever in the Garden (Heaven) or the Fire (Hell), although some theologians hold that Hell will eventually come to an end, and only Heaven will endure forever. The life of this world compared to the Hereafter is like a drop of water compared to the ocean. Muslim patients facing death remember, and are reminded by their family, friends and religious figures, that death is not the end of their lives, but merely a temporary phenomenon that everyone will 'taste', and that facing death is in fact preparing for a much longer lifetime ahead in the Hereafter.[24]

Another authoritative Islamic statement says:

Islamic Eschatology gives roles to Gog and Magog, the Mahdi, the Antichrist and to Jesus. Suddenly Jesus will appear, and with him the radical correction of the world, the opening of the doors of paradise and the doors of hell, and the discrimination of the spirits. With respect to individual eschatology, Islam, like all monotheistic traditions, has a sharp distinction between the posthumous states of paradise and hell. The Prophet said: 'When we live, we dream, and when we die, we wake.' Whether we are true to our real selves and to the Real – this is what determines our state after death. Identification with the Truth leads to paradise, and rejection to hell. However, those who are not perfected, but are without fundamental fault, may enter into a limbo, or the kind of intermediary state without suffering, as they undergo final purification, a state, which unfailingly opens on the state of the blessed..... The Prophet said 'Those who have merited paradise will enter it; the damned will go to hell. God will then say: Let those leave hell whose hearts contain even the weight of a mustard seed of faith! They will then be released, although they will already have been burned to ashes, and plunged into the river of rainwater, or into the river of life; and immediately they will be revived.' There is, finally, hell itself, which lasts in perpetuity – if not in eternity – until the extinction of the personality.... The Koran speaks of various paradises, each corresponding, no doubt, to different degrees of blessedness.... The human, or central state is distinguished from all others precisely because it is characterized by the capacity to know the Absolute. To be born human is therefore to arrive at a great crossroads. Islam simplifies the choice of direction into two main paths, because, ultimately, the consequences of being human are either that of becoming sanctified, or that of being reduced to the sub-human, whatever the modes. Damnation is the forfeit, or ultimate loss, of the human state because of revolt, disbelief, or, in the case of the 'indifferent' of simply abandoning the responsibility of being God's 'viceroy' on earth. Paradise is the realization of conformity to our true nature; closeness to God because of knowledge of Him; and salvation.[25]

These two extensive quotations from Islamic sources show the central role that judgment plays in Islamic thought, and the interesting notion that Jesus will be involved. A mainstream

Islamic belief relates to the *barzakh* (isthmus) between a person's death and the Day of Judgment, where Islam believes that each person experiences bliss or punishment in the grave. A popular Islamic belief is that one or two angels come to the person just after the moment of burial to ask questions about their faith, with Shia Muslims believing that the questions include which Imam the person followed. Depending on their answers constitutes whether they are rewarded or punished on the Day of Judgment; although this is not to be found in the Qur'an it is described in numerous *hadiths*, (statements or views made or approved by the Prophet in his lifetime). A general Sunni view is also that the deceased is aware and informed of the actions of his/her family.

John Bowker in his study of Islamic beliefs in *The Meanings of Death* also makes an important observation about what happens at the Day of Judgment with individuals being sent to Paradise (the Garden) or Hell (the Fire); "these descriptions, for the vast majority of Muslims, are not metaphorical; they describe literally (since the Qur'an is the word coming directly down from God) a part of his creation."[26] He concludes "Islam rests, as the other major religions do not, on one literal and inerrant picture of the final outcomes of human lives beyond death."[27]

However, while that may well be true of strictly orthodox Muslims there has been a broader intellectual tradition within Islam that may point to wider perspectives. Someone within the broad Islamic tradition wrote *The Rubayyat of Omar Khayyam*, although not much is known for certain about Omar Khayyam other than he was a mathematician and astronomer. It is believed his father was a convert to Islam from Zoroastrianism and Khayyam followed his father, although with a strong skeptical stance. There is an academic debate about the relationship of Khayyam to Sufism, a mystical version of Islam, but he retained a thoughtful perspective and in *The Rubayyat* expresses some of that questioning.

Why, all the Saints and Sages who discuss'd
Of the Two Worlds so learnedly, are thrust
Like foolish Prophets forth; their Works to Scorn
Are scatter'd, and their Mouths are stopt with dust.

Oh, come with old Khayyam, and leave the Wise
To talk; one thing is certain, that life flies:
One thing is certain, and the Rest is Lies;
The Flower that once had blown forever dies.[28]

That was written in the eleventh century and, it is said because of the doubts raised by his skepticism, Khayyam made a pilgrimage to Mecca to prove his commitment to Islam.

Such a broader approach is not unknown within Islam today, as well illustrated by Professor Lenn E Goodman:

"Islamic humanism has a long and splendid history. But if pursued as an option for today, it does not come ready made, and this book offers neither a recipe nor a prescription.... The task of forging a new and humanistic Islam lies with thoughtful and progressive Muslims."[29] The sacred and the secular, he writes "Islam, like every religion, harbors its own secular moments and spaces. It fosters secularities that are at once inimical to its claims yet symbiotic with it. They are dependent on it, but also supportive of its world presence and self-assertion. And they exact a price in distraction of gaze and diffusion of interests.... Islam becomes a way of life coloring every culture reached by the Qur'an and the Arabic language. In the cosmopolitan civilization that results, communities and individuals find their own tents and awning, accommodating the sacred and the secular in various modes of coexistence, some intricately devised, some casual or haphazard, some coherent, others restive or unstable, some synthetic or creative, others vapid, stiff or angry. Many of these shelters are such that those who have lived in their shade could find they were experiencing something of the best of this world without being deprived of some taste of the next."[30] On the rise of universal historiography he notes the work of one Islamic scholar, Ibn Khaldun, and says of it "Granted that the overarching framework of creation-history-judgment remains unquestioned and unquestionable for the most faithful adherents of Islam.... nonetheless, the idea that creation frames the most fundamental question for the historical and that the Day of Judgment frames the ultimate answer to that question is quietly but decisively set aside by Moslem historical writers. Even when their work rises far above the local and parochial, their standpoint is more earthbound than that. Judgment is sought *within* history, not just at its end. That is true even of Muhammad and of many others who took on the role... the search for a moral shape and thrust in history cunningly intertwines with the prophet before him. It is also true of our universal historians. Ibn Khaldun, drawing together the work of many predecessors, takes his problematic from the ways of life that he finds on earth. He finds the meaning that he seeks in history not in any final denouement but in the very cycles of power that fill the span of human life and mark the rise and falls of societies, as he knows them."[31]

It remains to be seen how what Goodman describes as "thoughtful and progressive Muslims" respond to the challenges to the notion of the soul raised for Christian theologians in the twentieth century by the science and philosophy described in later chapters.

Hinduism

There is a huge variety of religious approaches to death in Eastern religions, and, in complete contrast to Islam, Hinduism understands that diversity as a strength, not least because a number of texts embody different aspects of Hindu belief. According to one authority [32] in one of the earliest Hindu documents, the Regveda, which is a collection of ancient Vedic hymns, there is no mention of rebirth or reincarnation, but John Bowker suggests that the starting point should be the later Bhagavad Gita, which occurs within a long epic, the Mahabharata. It recounts a war between two branches of a family where one side goes to the extent of defying the manifestation of the God Vishnu in the form of Krishna. One of the sons of the other side, Arjuna, chooses to serve Krishna, but, at the moment when the Gita begins, has a crisis of conscience and refuses to fight as he says he cannot bring himself to kill his revered teachers and members of his own family. The main part of the Gita is taken up with Krishna's response to his paralysis. He maintains that Arjuna is giving a false importance to death, because the selves, which are embodied, are eternal and cannot therefore die when the body dies. Krishna is reported as saying "whoever thinks that the embodied self can be the one who kills, or can be killed, has no sound understanding. It does not kill nor can it be killed. It is not born, it does not die... As a person throws away his clothes when they are worn out and puts on new ones, so does the embodied self cast off its old bodies and enter new ones."[33] However, Bowker goes on to ask "Can one say, then, that the Gita is the Hindu understanding of death? Clearly not, because the Gita itself is open to very different interpretations. Although the Gita seems to envisage the final state as a relation with Krishna, and not as union with Brahman understood as the Absolute and undifferentiated source of all appearance, other interpretations nevertheless appear in both ancient and modern guise."[34] A further complication is that Sanskrit words used in the texts do not always have a direct translation into English. *Dharma* (duty), *atman* (the true self), *brahman* (the state experienced in liberation both in this life and after death), and *nirvana* (the state of happiness and peace of one who is eternally with Krishna) are each aspects of those four words, but they do not confine them, and in the case of nirvana, it represents a very different idea from the Buddhist one discussed below. In terms of popular Hinduism, it seems that reincarnation into another person or living thing is envisaged. "Souls are immortal and imperishable, so death is not a great calamity but a natural process in the existence of jiva (being) as a separate entity, a resting period during which it recuperates, reassembles its resources, adjusts its course and returns again to earth to continue its journey. In Hinduism, unless a soul is liberated, neither life nor afterlife is permanent. They are both part of a grand illusion." What happens to the soul after death depends on many factors; previous deeds (which may entail going to a lower world or to a higher sun-filled world to enjoy life there), the state of mind at the time of death (for example, someone thinking at the time of death of their family may come back as a future member of their family, or someone thinking of money may come back as a merchant or trader), the time of death (dying on a festival day may have the consequence of going straight to heaven), the activities of children in performing the funeral rites in their prescribed manner, and the grace of God. "It is maintained that the purpose of a future life is not to be punished or rewarded, but to remind the true purpose of their existence. The difference between heaven and hell is immaterial because both are part of the great illusion that characterizes the whole creation. The difference is very much like the difference between a good dream and a bad dream. It should not matter to a soul whether it has gone to a heaven or to some hell, because the soul is eternally pure and not subject to pain and suffering. It is the residual jiva, that part which leaves the body and goes to the higher planes after death, which is subject to the process of learning through pain and pleasure in the temporary worlds of heaven and hell. Once its learning is accomplished and the effects of its previous karma is exhausted it returns to the earth to continue its existence."[35]

Because Hinduism believes in individual souls, nirvana is perceived as the final resting place of the soul where it is liberated from the cycle of birth and death through self-knowledge and in eternal union with the metaphysical Brahman. This is in contrast to Buddhism.

Buddhism

Buddhism is a non-theistic religion, but it also has varieties within it. According to John Bowker, Theravada Buddhism (mainly in Sri Lanka and South East Asia) claims to have stayed closer to the teaching of the Buddha. Mahayana Buddhism took root mainly in Tibet, Korea, China and Japan.

Gautama, who became the Buddha, started life in a palace protected by his father from encountering anything that might be disturbing. However, one day he asked his carriage-driver to take him out of the palace and he encountered the sufferings of ordinary people including a dead body being prepared for cremation. He then encountered an ascetic, wearing a saffron robe, who was anticipating death by practicing detachment from all worldly entanglements in this life. Gautama left his palace, abandoning his wife and son, and embraced many of the methods of austerity and detachments available in the Indian religions of the time (sixth century BCE). But that austerity did not bring any final relief. It may postpone death, but it cannot rescue some inner reality into a condition immune from death. That led Gautama to the point of Enlightenment, when he understood that there is nothing – no thing – which is not subject to transience, change and dissolution. There is not even a self, an *atmen* or soul, which continues from life to life through the repetition of death: there is no-self (*anatta*); only the process of change which produces apparent forms.[36]

This represented a significant change from Hinduism. The German scholar Helmuth von Glasenapp summarized the distinction:[37] "The Atman doctrine of the Vedanta and the Dharma theory of Buddhism exclude each other. The Vedanta tries to establish an Atman as the basis of everything, whilst Buddhism maintains that everything in the empirical world is only a stream of passing Dharmas (impersonal and evanescent processes) which therefore has to be characterized as Anatta, i.e., being without a persisting self, without independent existence."

The Buddha rejected an "eternalist" view, which in the Buddhist sense means a belief in an individual, eternal soul that survives death, but he also rejected the nihilist view that there is no existence for any of us beyond this one and this brought him to the Middle Way, which was a path to enlightenment that lay between the extremes of self-indulgence and self-denial.

He outlined the Four Noble Truths. The first, *dhukkha*, diagnoses the disease, discovering life as stressful, unsatisfying and sometimes involving suffering. This does not mean that everything in life is awful, the Buddha spoke of many forms of human happiness, but ultimately we find life unsatisfying. The second explains the cause of the disease; *dhukkha* is generated by craving, desire and even greed. The third describes the remedy, a cure, which is not easy to find, but involves learning not to grasp after our cravings and desires. The Fourth Noble Truth is the eightfold path:

The Wisdom Path,
    Right view or understanding
    Right Intention
The Ethical Conduct Path
    Right Speech
    Right Action
    Right Livelihood

The Mental Discipline Path
  Right Effort
  Right Mindfulness
  Right Concentration

The Four Nobles Truths are not simply to be read, they are to be lived. That relates to the Buddhist notion of karma. The Sanskrit word means "volitional act" or "deed." The law of karma is a law of cause and effect, or an understanding that every deed produces fruit. In Buddhism, karma is *not* a cosmic criminal justice system. There is no intelligence behind it that is rewarding or punishing. It's more like a Law of Nature. Karma is created by the *intentional* acts of body, speech, and mind.

In most schools of Buddhism, it's understood that the effects of karma, cause and effect are simultaneous. It's also the case that once set in motion, karma tends to continue in many directions, like ripples on a pond. So, whether you believe in rebirth or not, karma is still important. What you do now impacts the life you are living now. Karma is not mysterious or hidden. Once you understand what it is, you can observe it all around you. For example, a man gets into an argument at work. He drives home in an angry mood, cutting off someone at an intersection. The driver cut off is now angry, and when she gets home she yells at her daughter. This is karma in action – one angry act has touched off many more. However, if the man who argued had the mental discipline to let go of his anger, the karma would have stopped with him. Karma can lead to happiness or unhappiness.

While the Buddhist notion of reincarnation does not involve the transmigration of any individual soul, it does hold that when someone dies the energy generated by their karma does survive and passes on to someone else at their birth. At the end of what may be a very long process of karma being passed from one individual to another the final conclusion for a genuinely enlightened one is Nirvana. The Buddha told his monks that

Nirvana cannot be imagined, and so there is no point speculating what it is like. Even so, it is a word that Buddhists use, and Nirvana is not a place, but rather a state of being beyond existence and non-existence. The early sutras speak of nirvana as "liberation" and "unbinding," meaning no longer being bound to the cycle of birth and death. Theravada Buddhism recognizes two kinds of nirvana. An enlightened being enjoys a kind of provisional nirvana, or "nirvana with remainders." He or she is still aware of pleasure and pain but is not bound to them. The enlightened individual enters into parinirvana, or complete nirvana at death. In Theravada, then, enlightenment is spoken of as the door to nirvana, but not nirvana itself.[38]

The Notion of Reincarnation

The Hindu view of reincarnation may well make it attractive for many, but there remains the question of whether it is credible. Some have certainly asserted that it is, giving examples of people who believed they knew who they were before and knew facts about their previous lives. A more skeptical view, however, would point out that the vast majority of people do not remember their so-called previous lives and there is no clear evidence of any mechanism that allows personality to survive death. The Wikipedia article on reincarnation suggests that "positing the existence of reincarnation is subject to the principle that extraordinary claims require extraordinary evidence."[39] Many recent philosophers and scientists would certainly question the very notion of an immortal and imperishable soul which I outline in the section on Cartesian dualism in a later chapter.

The Buddhist view is more difficult to assess, as it does not assume any progress of individual souls. The Rev. Takashi Tsuji, a Jodo Shinshu priest, wrote about belief in reincarnation:

It is said that the Buddha left 84,000 teachings; the symbolic figure represents the diverse backgrounds characteristics, tastes, etc. of the people. The Buddha taught according to the mental and spiritual capacity of each individual. For the simple village folks living during the time of the Buddha, the doctrine of reincarnation was a powerful moral lesson. Fear of birth into the animal world must have frightened many people from acting like animals in this life. If we take this teaching literally today we are confused because we cannot understand it rationally.... A parable, when taken literally, does not make sense to the modern mind. Therefore we must learn to differentiate the parables and myths from actuality.

While, therefore, some more popular Buddhist beliefs about reincarnation might be subject to the same criticisms as the Hindu belief, the more sophisticated ideas may be difficult to dismiss, although exactly how the energy of one person's karma mysteriously becomes present in another new-born infant is not clear. The Dalai Lama once said that it was scientifically impossible to disprove reincarnation. That obviously depends on the meaning of reincarnation.

Conclusion

As will have been evident there have been and still are a wide variety of conceptions of what might constitute life after death in the various religions of the world, including doubt about any sort of afterlife expressed by the Sadducees in Judaism and many of the philosophers of ancient Greece. We must now move to consider the development of the notion within the Christian tradition prior to the twentieth century.

Chapter 1 Endnotes

1 Hariri YN. *Homo Deus. A Brief History of Tomorrow.* Vintage, a part of the Penguin Random House group; 2015. p. 15.
2 p. 31.
3 Vermes G. *The Authentic Gospel of Jesus.* The Folio Society; 2009. p. 73.
4 This quotation comes from a Facebook discussion group, from which Rabbi Solomon has kindly given me permission to quote.
5 Rabbi Helen Freeman, of the West London Synagogue, which is a Reform Synagogue.
6 Kenny A. *A New History of Ancient Philosophy* Volume 1. OUP; 2004. p. 229.
7 Kenny. p. 231.
8 Kenny. p. 35f.
9 Kenny. p. 234.
10 Plato. *Phaedo.* Translation with commentary by David Gallop. OUP; 1975. 64c.
11 p. 66b and 66d.
12 p. 109.
13 Kenny. p. 237.
14 West, T G. *Plato's Apology of Socrates: An Interpretation with a New Translation.* Cornell University Press; 1979. pp. 47–49.
15 Kenny. p. 242.
16 Aristotle. *De Anima (On the Soul).* Translated by Hugh Lawson-Tancred. Penguin Classics; 1986. p. 158.
17 p. 158.
18 Phaedo. 70a.
19 The letter is available on the website epicurus.net.
20 Seneca. *How to Die: An Ancient Guide to the End of Life.* Translated by James S Romm. Princeton University Press; 2018. p. 13.
21 Hussain AA. 'Ensoulment and the prohibition of Abortion in Islam'. Al-Mahadi Institute working papers; 2016. No 4.

22 Qur'an 7.172.

23 Qur'an 3.185.

24 Husan U. Health, sickness, medicine, life and death in Muslim belief and practice. *European Journal of Palliative Care*. 2012; 19(5) p. 241.

25 Glasse C. *The Concise Encyclopedia of Islam*. London: Stacey International; 1989.

26 Bowker J. *The Meanings of Death*. First published by CUP in 1991, Canto edition 1993. p. 118.

27 Bowker. p. 128.

28 *The Rubayyat of Omar Khayyam*. London: RHS publications; 1969.p. 23 quatrains XXVII and XXVIII.

29 Goodman LE. *Islamic Humanism*. OUP; 2003. p. 28.

30 *Islamic Humanism*. p. 81.

31 *Islamic Humanism*. p. 209f.

32 Hinduwebsite.com/Death and Afterlife in Hinduism.

33 Bowker. pp. 132–3.

34 Bowker. p. 135f.

35 Hinduwebsite.com/Death and Afterlife.

36 Bowker. p. 169f.

37 In a comparative study of Vedanta (a major branch of Hinduism) and Buddhism (*Akademie der Wissenschaften and Literatur*, 1950).

38 Much of this whole section on Buddhism can be found on ThoughtCo.com with articles including "What do Buddhists Believe" and "Buddhist Teachings on Reincarnation and Rebirth" by Barbara O'Brien, an author and journalist who has written extensively on Buddhism.

39 Wikipedia/ Reincarnation.

Chapter 2

Christianity prior to the Twentieth Century

Christianity emerged from a Jewish background so some of the notions about death flowed from that, but by the time of Jesus there had already been developments within the original Jewish view as shown in the last chapter. The New Testament gives a complicated picture of "the last things." Many believe Paul's first letter to the Thessalonians was written in the year 52 CE, and there he appears to envisage a return of Jesus in the lifetime of some of those alive at the time. However, even with Paul that view was not evident in all his later letters, and there appears to have been a gradual development while the New Testament was being written from such an immanent belief in the return of Christ into something more long term and into the future. That is most clearly seen in the Fourth Gospel, although even there in Chapter 21 there is a suggestion that maybe Jesus would return before the death of the beloved disciple, but the more common interpretation of that Gospel is that it showed Christ could be already seen in the life of the church in a "realized eschatology" before any final "return."

Certainly, a belief in the resurrection permeated the whole New Testament, although what might have happened to provoke that belief will be considered in the next chapter. But the close of the New Testament did not see the end of reflection on what the future might hold for Christians and ultimately for the world as a whole. Over two thousand years of Christian history that has been worked out in a variety of Christian doctrines against the background of changing philosophical fashions, and at least since the Enlightenment against developing historical and scientific knowledge. As it applies to the Christian doctrine of the last things it has been well documented in *Afterlife: A History of Life after Death* by Philip C. Almond[1] and also in *The Christian Hope* by Brian Hebblethwaite.[2] In both cases I happen to disagree with their final conclusions, but as overall descriptions of two thousand years of Christian thought they provide valuable reviews.

In this chapter my main concern is with Christian discussion about any afterlife before the beginning of the twentieth century. This is certainly not the comprehensive survey of that whole period that Almond and Hebblethwaite provide, but I note some influential figures whose thoughts, while developed in times very different from our own, had a lasting significance.

Origen (c185–254 CE)

Origen was one of the most prolific and independent theologians of the early church, serving in the Christian Catechetical School in Alexandria, possibly as head, and later in Caesarea. While never formally denying anything in scripture he was certainly prepared to speculate beyond its bounds. For example, on belief about the resurrection of individual Christians he did not believe in a literal, physical resurrection, but the replacement of a fleshly body by a spiritual body, which perhaps reflected his sympathy with Platonic thought. His view was certainly not shared at the time by many of his fellow Christians, even though it could be construed from St Paul's comments in I Corinthians 15.44 about being "raised a spiritual body" and in 15.50 about "flesh and blood not inheriting the kingdom of God." It was a debate that would be continued for many years in the life of the church.

Origen also contributed to another discussion relating to eschatology, which continued long after his death. The New Testament refers to Hades and Gehenna, using the first as simply meaning the place of the departed and the latter as a place of punishment. Translators from the Greek did not always observe that distinction, with Hades often translated as "hell." As Almond puts it "It is little wonder that theorizing about the afterlife using those translations could get messy."[3] Origen, however, did observe that distinction, suggesting "when Christ descended into Hades to preach to those dwelling there, those who were not converted descended further into Gehenna for punishment."[4] Even more remarkably he envisaged a form of universal salvation, for of the phrase "the last enemy shall be destroyed" he wrote "His destruction means not his ceasing to exist but ceasing to be an enemy and ceasing to be death. Nothing is impossible to omnipotence; there is nothing that cannot be healed by its Maker."[5] Hebblethwaite comments "thus we encounter the most remarkable instance of Christian universalism in early Church theology. Such universalism,... implicit only in certain strands of the New Testament, is here brought out and developed to its logical conclusion. This view was exceptional, and much criticized at the time and indeed throughout the fourth century."

As we shall see hell as a place of eternal punishment featured extensively in much medieval thinking so Origen's caution about aspects of it at such an early stage of Christian thought was striking. His thoughts about hell only came to hold a stronger position much later in Christian development, but it does show that even at that early stage Christian thought was open to a variety of interpretations.

St Augustine of Hippo (354–430 CE)

While Origen was probably the most speculative of theologians, St Augustine was the most influential at least until the time of St Thomas Aquinas. As a young man Augustine was attracted to Manichaeism but then converted to Christianity while in Milan and he was baptized in 387. While there he came under the influence of the Bishop of Milan, Ambrose, who was himself influenced by a form of Neo-Platonism, which also made a great impression on Augustine. He returned to Africa, was ordained priest in 391 and then Bishop of Hippo in 395 and he remained in that post until his death in 430. He wrote extensively, including his autobiographical *Confessions* and his major work *City of God*, written in response to the sack of Rome by the Visigoths in 410 and the allegation that Christianity brought about the decline of Rome. It was written over many years and contains 22 books and it was, and remains for some still, a very influential philosophical and theological work written with style and clarity. He was canonized by popular acclaim and this was formally recognized when he was declared a doctor of the church in 1298.

In Book VIII Augustine wrote "Among the disciples of Socrates it was Plato who deservedly achieved the most outstanding reputation, and he quite overshadowed all the rest." He says he will refer to much of Plato's work and "Sometimes these quotations support the true religion, which our faith has received and now defends; sometimes they seem to show him in opposition to it. There are passages concerning the question of the divine unity or plurality with reference to life after death, which is the life of true blessedness. There are thinkers who have rightly recognized Plato's pre-eminence over the pagan philosophers and have won praise for the perception and accuracy of their judgment, and enjoy a widespread reputation as his followers."[6] Augustine's view of Platonism was not therefore an unqualified acceptance of everything it claimed, but he did fuse a relationship between the Christian Faith and Platonism that was to last for many centuries.

On the matter of "the death of the soul and the death of the body" he wrote in Book XIII:

For though the human soul is rightly described as immortal, it has nevertheless a kind of death of its own. It is said to be immortal for this reason that it never entirely ceases to live and to feel, even if only in the slightest degree. The body, on the other hand, is mortal in that it can be completely bereft of life, and by itself it has no life of any sort. The death of the soul results when God abandons it, the death of the body when the soul departs. Therefore the death of the whole man, of both these elements, comes about when the soul, abandoned by God, leaves the body. For then the soul no longer derives life from God, nor does the body receive life from the soul.

However, he goes on to write:

It may seem strange that the body is said to be killed by a death in which it is not abandoned by the soul, but remains possessed of soul and feeling, and endures torment in this condition. For in that final and everlasting punishment ... we correctly talk of 'the death of the soul', because it no longer derives life from God. But how can we talk in this case of the death of the body, since it is deriving life from the soul? For otherwise it cannot feel the bodily torments which are to follow the resurrection. Is it because life of any kind is a good thing, while pain is an evil, and for this reason the body cannot be said to be alive, when the purpose of the soul is not the body's life, but the body's pain? The soul therefore derives life from God, when its life is good – for a life cannot be good except when God is active in it to produce what is good – while the body derives life from the soul when the soul is alive in the body, whether the body derives its life from God or not. For the life of the bodies of the ungodly is not the life of their souls but of their bodies, a life which souls can confer even when their souls are dead, that is when God abandons them; for their own life, in virtue of which they are immortal, still persists, in however low a degree.

But in this last condemnation ... what he feels is the anguish of punishment, and so his condition is rightly called death rather than life. The second death is so called because it follows the first, in which there is a separation of natures, which cohere together, either God and the soul, or the soul and the body. It can therefore be said of the first death that it is good for the good, bad for the bad; but the second death does not happen to any of the good, and without doubt it is not good for anyone.[7]

In the final Book 22 he discusses at length the nature of resurrection bodies taking the example of the risen body of Jesus. He considered the problem when wild beasts destroyed someone's body, or when it was destroyed by fire or even by cannibalism. He commented "It is unthinkable that the Creator should lack the power to revive them all and restore them to life"[8] and went on to consider the size, maturity and even the nature of the resurrected body.

In the resurrection of the body for eternal life the body will have the size and dimensions which it had attained, or was to attain, at maturity, according to the design implanted in the body of each person, with its appropriate beauty preserved also in proportion of all the parts. If, in order to preserve this beauty, something has been taken from a part displeasing by excessive size, and if this is dispersed throughout the whole body, in such a way that this material is not lost, while the congruence of the parts is kept, then there is no absurdity in believing that there may be some addition to the stature of the body as a result of this, provided that the material is so distributed to all the parts as to preserve the beauty of the whole, which would be spoilt if it were concentrated disproportionately in one place. On the other hand, if it is maintained that every person is to rise again with the precise stature he had when he departed this life, there is no occasion for violent opposition to such an opinion, provided only that all ugliness must disappear, all weakness, all sluggishness, all corruption, and anything else that is inconsistent with that kingdom in which the sons of resurrection and of the promise will be equal to the angels of God, in felicity if not in body or in age.[9]

The modern reader might find it extraordinary that Augustine should go into such detail, but his thought was to be a significant part in the beliefs of Christians over many centuries. Whether it remains credible for contemporary Christians and others is, of course, another matter.

St Thomas Aquinas (1225–1274)

St Thomas Aquinas was born several centuries after Augustine and after his death was canonized some 50 years later as a doctor of the church in 1323. Contrary to the wishes of his family he became a Dominican Friar. In that capacity he devoted his life to philosophy, theology and related subjects. Anthony Kenny describes him as "one of the dozen greatest philosophers of the western world." Although he did not reject every aspect of the Platonism that Augustine sympathized with, a major part of Thomas' work was to fuse a link between Christianity and Aristotelian thought.

His understanding of God is perhaps the most valuable contribution he made to theological understanding. Aquinas believed that grace perfects nature, and he distinguished between knowledge that was obtainable by natural reason, and knowledge that came through revelation. Natural reason for Aquinas led to belief in God, although his view of God was more complex than the God so often dismissed today. In the Prologue to his major work *Summa Theologiae* he stated "We do not know what God is but what he is not."

Fergus Kerr sums up Aquinas' view:

God is not a body, like a planet, as many at the time no doubt imagined... Thomas had his eye on something more sophisticated. God is not a substance with accidents, a being with properties – as creatures are. God *is* what he *has* – a much trickier thesis. That is to say: such characteristics as goodness, truth, eternity, and so on are not attributes that qualify God's being. That would make God's essence subject to modification and therefore incomplete. God is not to be envisaged as a substance with accidents, an entity with an array of qualities. God is omniscient, not in virtue of instantiating or exemplifying omniscience – which would imply a real distinction between God's nature and his omniscience. The properties that are attributed in the Bible to God – wisdom, justice, mercy, love and so on – are not properties in the sense of being added on to, or in principle separable from, God's being. These evidently disparate qualities have to be conceived as identical, in the divine case. We are forced to say this, Thomas thinks, because the alternative would be to make God some kind of creature. To speak of the 'simpleness' of the divine nature is to deny of God any of the distinctions that characterize created things, especially, of course, ourselves. In short, God is not to be perceived anthropomorphically.... God is in everything, 'not as a part or a property but like the agent in an action' (ST 1.8); God is not subject to being changed by anything external to himself: nothing is eternal to God (ST 1.9); God is not subject to time or temporal change (ST 1.10). Finally, God is unique, singular: otherwise something would be alongside God, constraining him (ST 1.11).[10]

Kerr comments "These are standard claims in ancient Christian theology, conveniently and compactly set out – by no means uncontested in modern times." Among those contested claims today might be how Aquinas understands the notion of God as Creator. As I have quoted elsewhere Martin Rees, the Astronomer Royal, in his book *Our Cosmic Habitat* wrote "The pre-eminent mystery is why anything exists at all."[11] Thomas suggested that "God" is certainly not a creature in the universe that may or may not exist. "God" may simply be the word we use for why there is anything at all. That does not imply that we should ignore what cosmologists can tell us about the origins of the universe, and neither should we assume that God is an agent in the world other than through the natural processes of development that we can discern in the universe about us, and in his influence on those who believe in him. Both those issues were considered in the twentieth century, as, inevitably given the history of that century, was whether we can easily speak of God not suffering. As Bonheoffer wrote "Only a suffering God can help." But understanding such fundamental matters as truth, goodness and beauty may be rooted in the very meaning of God gives the notion of God significance even in our contemporary and more skeptical world.

From Aristotle, Aquinas also understood the soul to be the form of the body and the body was the matter of the soul. It was the soul that made inanimate things living beings. While Thomas believed the soul could survive without a body, so he had a notion of the soul as incorporeal and immaterial, yet he also believed that the soul and the body required a final reunion in order to enjoy eternal life. He therefore envisaged a final resurrection where the blessed would enjoy the Beatific Vision, but he also paid attention to what he saw as the biblical revelation which included the notion of an eternal punishment and the pains of hell. On aspects of that he was quite specific. "For those in hell receive diverse punishments according to the diversity of their guilt, so that those who are condemned are consigned to darker and deeper parts of hell according as they have been guilty of graver sins."[12] Philip Almond says that Thomas had a fourfold division of hell.

One hell was a place of the damned, an abode in which

the damned were both denied the vision of God and were physically tormented. Above that was another hell, a place of darkness without the vision of God but without physical torments. This hell ... is called 'the Limbo of the Children.' Above the Limbo of the Children was a further place of darkness without the vision of God but which did nonetheless include physical suffering (but from which release was possible). This ... was called 'Purgatory'. Finally, above Purgatory, there was yet another hell. This too was a place of darkness without the vision of God, yet again without physical torments. This was the 'hell of the holy fathers'. It was to this region of hell, he remarked, that Christ had descended between his death and his resurrection: he had gone no further.[13]

Hebblethwaite commented on Thomas' teaching about hell: "For Thomas Aquinas the fate of the damned was fixed at death.... They would immediately experience the fires of hell. Even more tortuous arguments were required to show how disembodied souls could suffer from physical fire! There is no need for us to go into these implausible aspects of the great doctor's teaching."[14]

Thomas' belief in purgatory and limbo was very influential in his time, but as with Augustine's view, whether it can be credible for today is precisely the issue at stake.

Dante Alighieri (1265–1321)

Dante's *The Divine Comedy* is a long poem written in about the last twelve years of his life. Unusually for his time he wrote in Italian rather than Latin and its imaginative picture of Hell, Purgatory and Heaven exercised a great influence in medieval Europe. For a period it went out of fashion, but it was revived in the Romantic era in the late eighteenth and early nineteenth centuries.

While it is clearly an imaginary work with many Christian

notions, it also incorporates a wide variety of other figures and images from history. Dante's guide through Hell and Purgatory was the pre-Christian Roman poet Virgil and together, after passing the gate above which was written "Abandon hope, all ye who enter here" they visited the nine circles of hell, starting with limbo, which for Dante included unbaptized children, worthy figures from the Old Testament and virtuous pagans and then each lower level becoming grimmer than the one before. In moving from the fifth to the sixth level of hell, Dante includes Greek and Roman myths as they cross the river Styx, he then encounters the final four circles of hell in the eighth of which are to be found various Popes; the final circle is reserved for traitors to God and the Empire.

He and Virgil then move to climb the mount of Purgatory, where on seven terraces sinners expiate the seven deadly sins, being encouraged to adopt the opposite virtue, until finally they arrive in a sacred forest at the top of the mount. There Dante takes his leave of Virgil and moves through the forest until he encounters his guide for paradise, Beatrice, who as a child in Florence, Dante had loved, but who had died in 1290.

In Dante's image, paradise also has nine concentric circles represented by different planets starting with the moon and on his journey through those various heavens and planets he talks with various saintly figures, including in the fourth heaven Thomas Aquinas. Finally, he encounters St Bernard, who supplicates the Virgin Mary that he might contemplate the Divine Majesty and glimpse the greatest mystery, the Trinity, and the Union of man with God.

Hebblethwaite comments on the whole tradition of medieval theology including Aquinas and Dante: "No modern theologian, trained in the critical study of the Bible and Christian tradition would suppose that we are in a position to set out the destiny of humankind as precisely and in such detail as Thomas Aquinas thought he could. But even the general features of medieval eschatology contain some theologically implausible elements."[15] He accepts that there had been an abandonment of the idea of two resurrections, but it was still committed to belief in two judgments, the particular judgment at death and the general judgment at the coming of Christ in the general resurrection. He believes later theologians tried to work out a more unified picture of human destiny. That will be the subject of a later chapter.

Martin Luther (1483–1546)

Luther retained the overall view of the last things as involving resurrection, judgment, hell and heaven, but his opposition to the Catholic practice of selling indulgences to avoid the pains of purgatory was the major initial factor in the revolution in European Christianity that was the Reformation. Luther rejected any notion that the Pope could control a human being's future destiny, and in the process of challenging that he rediscovered St Paul's emphasis on faith as the means of accepting God's offer of justifying grace. That was decisive in Luther's understanding of eschatology; accepting grace through faith was the point when a human being encountered the reality of eternity. There was therefore no place for any intermediate state such as purgatory or even limbo. He also recognized that in this world there are two Kingdoms, the kingdom of Christ, where Christians live by faith in the knowledge of God-given righteousness, and the kingdom of this world, where rulers accept a responsibility for the life of the whole community. In the kingdom of this world he was content to see secular rulers as the agents of God's sovereignty.

John Calvin (1509–64)

Calvin put more emphasis on hope for a final resurrection as the point when the rule of Christ would be seen. He encouraged Christians to meditate on the future life "as part of the life and exercise of daily faith." But he was more confident than Luther in the historical mission of the visible Church, and more confident in the positive role of the Church in the ordering of human life in general.

But it was his conviction that God's sovereign will was absolute that produced the most influential, but for many the most disturbing, aspect of his teaching about the last things; double predestination – some to salvation and some to eternal damnation. He wrote in *The Institutes of the Christian Religion* "As scripture clearly shows we say that God once established by his eternal and unchangeable plan those whom he long before determined once for all to receive into salvation, and those whom, on the other hand, he would devote to destruction. We assert that, with respect to the elect, this plan was founded upon his freely given mercy, without regard to human worth; but by his just and incomprehensible judgment he has barred the door to life to those whom he has given over to damnation."[16] To be predestined for damnation does not, for many, seem to be the act of a loving God. Hebblethwaite comments "It is hard enough to hold the view that the glory of God is equally subserved by the bliss of the redeemed and by the suffering of the damned; but, if both those states are results of divine decree, then such a doctrine of God's sovereignty is morally incredible."[17]

René Descartes (1596–1660)

One consequence of the Reformation, particularly in reaction to the wars of religion fought during it, was to search for a more tolerant way of human beings living together. Coupled with that was the recognition that conflicting views of revelation had exacerbated the conflicts of the Reformation, and human beings had to look to other ways of reflecting on truth. Those factors provided the stimulus for the intellectual movement started in the seventeenth century known as the Enlightenment, where reason rather than revelation was taken as the starting point. Those who advocated it were secular philosophers rather than theologians, although that certainly did not mean they were automatically opposed to religion. There certainly were critics of religion within the Enlightenment; David Hume would be the prime British example, but others were certainly not, and among them was René Descartes.

Descartes was a French philosopher and mathematician who is sometimes described as "the father of modern philosophy." Although he remained a Catholic throughout his life and argued for the existence of God, the starting point of his philosophy was not religious revelation of any form but rather "never to accept anything for true which I did not clearly know to be such; that is to say, carefully to avoid precipitancy and prejudice, and to comprise nothing more in my judgment than what was presented to my mind so clearly and distinctly as to exclude all ground of doubt."[18]

That led him to his most famous dictum "I think, therefore I am." (*Cogito ergo sum.*) For Descartes, the essence of being a human being is that an individual thinks, and he applied that not only to rational logical thinking but to all thinking that occurs in a person's consciousness. That was the fundamental principle from which his whole philosophical thought developed and he deduced that human beings consisted of two distinct parts, a body and a mind. The body was the obviously physical thing that existed in space and time, and which moves, breathes, and eats, while the mind results in thought and consciousness. For him, the union of the two was a union of two distinct substances; mind, which belonged to a private world that is inaccessible to others, and body, which inhabits the material world. He also concluded that the two are linked together through the pineal gland.

Although the pineal gland part of his theory did not last long, the notion that mind and body are two distinct parts of human beings continued, with the idea that, while the body obviously died, the mind might survive death and continue, possibly in some disembodied sense. The view is normally described as Cartesian dualism and it retained a powerful hold on popular imagination until it came under substantial criticism in the twentieth century, first from philosophy and later from science, and particularly neuroscience.

In the nineteenth century Darwin's theory of evolution probably had a bigger influence on Christian debate on most matters than any thought about the end of time, although Darwin himself and Thomas Huxley, one of the strongest proponents of Darwin's view, both professed themselves agnostic about any notion of life after death. It is also often assumed that from that time a clear disagreement emerged between scientific and Christian views, but in fact Christianity itself was quite divided on how to view evolution. Frederick Temple, who was to become Archbishop of Canterbury at the end of the nineteenth century gave lectures in Exeter Diocese when he was Bishop there in 1884 where he stated "the doctrine of evolution is in no sense whatever antagonistic to the teachings of Religion." However, as Philip Almond notes "At the turn of the twentieth century, Darwinian agnosticism was to segue, in the face of scientific materialism, into philosophical certainty."[19]

But that was not the whole picture. Anthony Kenny, who himself wrote a book against Cartesian Dualism, nonetheless wrote in his *History of Western Philosophy*,

Descartes' system was dualist, that is to say, it was tantamount to belief in two separate worlds – the physical world containing matter, and a psychical world containing private mental events. The two worlds are defined and described in such systematically different ways that mental and physical can interact, if at all, only in a mysterious manner that transcends the normal rules of causality and evidence. Such dualism is a fundamentally mistaken philosophy. The incoherence ... was to be pointed out with exhaustive patience in later centuries by Kant and Wittgenstein. But Cartesian dualism is still alive and well in the twenty-first century.[20]

Conclusion

Over the period of two millennia Christianity was in contact with a wide variety of philosophical traditions that certainly influenced how Christians came to think about any notion of what happened after death. From the perspective of the twenty-first century some certainly seem at the very least debatable and even unbelievable. But throughout that whole period the tradition of the resurrection of Jesus was a constant theme. It is to that, therefore, and some recent scholarship about it, we must now turn.

Chapter 2 Endnotes

1   Almond PC. *Afterlife: A History of Life After Death.* I.B. Tauris; 2016.

2   Hebblethwaite, B. *The Christian Hope.* (Revised Edition). OUP; 2010.

3   Almond p. 23.

4   Almond p. 23.

5   Origen. *De Principiis* III.vi.5 quoted by Hebblethwaite p. 45.

6   St Augustine. *The City of God.* Penguin Classics reissued 2003. p. 303 & 304.

7   pp. 510–511.

8   p. 1062.

9   p. 1063f.

10 Kerr F. *Thomas Aquinas: A Very Short Introduction.* OUP; 2009. pp. 41–43.

11 Rees M. *Our Cosmic Habitat.* Weidenfeld and Nicholson; 2002. p. 1 quoted in Reiss, R. *Sceptical Christianity.* Jessica Kingsley; 2016. p. 43.

12 Almond PC. *Afterlife: A History of Life after Death.* I B Tauris; 2016. p. 42f.

13 ibid p. 29.

14 Hebblethwaite p. 57f.

15 p. 67.

16 Calvin J. *Institutes of the Christian Religion.* The definitive edition was published in 1559. Now available edited by John T McNeill. London, Westminster: John Knox Press; 2006.

17 p. 73.

18 Descartes R. *Discourse on Method.* Harvard Classics; 1910.

19 p. 178.

20 Kenny A. *The Rise of Modern Philosophy: Volume 3 of A New History of Western Philosophy.* Clarendon Press; 2006. p. 219.

Chapter 3

Jesus' Resurrection

Any Christian thought must take account of the stories of the resurrection of Jesus and this chapter will consider them, but it must also take account of the contemporary life of the church. I saw clear evidence of the resurrection of Jesus in Southwark Cathedral in 2018, not on Easter Sunday as I was not there, but on Good Friday. As happens in many cathedrals and churches, part of the service included the Veneration of the Cross, when members of the congregation were invited to make their way to a Cross erected at the front of the nave and to kneel before it as an act of veneration. Along with many in the quite large congregation I did so, and what was completely evident is that for most if not all of those who participated this was an act of genuine devotion to an historical event that happened nearly 2000 years ago. The extraordinary act of self-sacrifice that was the crucifixion was clearly of profound importance for those who went forwards in that service, and while each individual's interpretation of it might have varied, nonetheless it revealed that the memory and example of Jesus then was for them of deep and continuing significance today.

That, I suggest, is what is most important about belief in the resurrection now. Jesus and all that he stood for in his life and death remains a motivating factor and example in the way countless people throughout the world live their lives.

But what of the original events that gave rise to the belief in resurrection?[1] The evidence of the New Testament, although it is confusing, can be stated quite clearly, and what may be of significance is to note when the various books that give accounts of it were written. The dating of those books is itself a matter of much debate. In 1976 Bishop John Robinson, by then Dean of

Trinity College, Cambridge wrote a book called *The Re-dating of the New Testament*, when he suggested much earlier dates for most of the New Testament books from the conventions of the time. It led to the wry comment of the then Master of Trinity, Lord R. A. Butler "I see the Dean of Chapel has written a book that says the whole of the New Testament was written before Jesus was born." In fact, it was not as extreme as that!

The thesis of Robinson's book may still have some supporters, but not many have accepted it and the dates given for the authorship of the New Testament books in this chapter are taken from the *Oxford Companion to the Bible*, published by Oxford University Press in 1993. It gave the dates that were the general consensus of academic scholarship then and I do not think they have altered significantly since. Wikipedia gives similar dates although with a broader range of possibilities and individual scholars might have their own views. It should be recognized that a book may well tell of events that were well known before they were written, but the form of the telling of the story tells us something about the state of mind of those who wrote at the time, and what will become evident is that over the sixty or more years from the crucifixion, probably between the years 30 and 33 CE, to the writing of the latest of the gospels probably after 90 CE there were significant developments in the story that was told.

One obvious fact should also be noted at the outset, the original authors were not writing in the way a twenty-first-century historian or even accurate journalist would write today. They could not easily consult sources written at the time of the actual events in the way that scholars would now and in all probability none of the authors knew the historical Jesus during his lifetime, although some might have known people who had. But their primary purpose was to foster and encourage belief in Jesus, hence their title Evangelists. This does not imply that they were deliberately writing things they knew to be untrue, but they were telling their stories with a purpose that was not purely or even primarily historical.

The earliest accounts to be written about the resurrection were in the letters of St Paul. In the Epistle to the Galatians, which may have been written as early as 46 CE and certainly by 55 CE, Paul tells of his own conversion. "I would have you know, brethren, that the gospel which was preached to me is not man's gospel. For I did not receive it from man, nor was I taught it, but it came through a revelation of Jesus Christ.... But when he who had set me apart before I was born, and had called me through his grace, was pleased to reveal his Son to me, in order that I might preach him among the Gentiles" (Gal. 1. 11–16). Later in that chapter he says he went to Jerusalem and there met Peter (whom he also knew as Cephas) and James, the brother of Jesus, so he at least had second-hand knowledge from those who certainly had known Jesus, but what is striking about his Galatians' statement is how brief it was about his own experience – "was pleased to reveal his Son to me." He gives no indication of what it was that he saw.

Much the same can be said of the statement in I Corinthians 15, probably written about 55 CE. Paul starts by giving what he had received from others: "That Christ died for our sins in accordance with the scriptures, and that he was buried, and he was raised on the third day in accordance with the scriptures, and that he appeared to Cephas, then to the twelve. Then he appeared to more than five hundred brethren at one time, most of whom are still alive although some have fallen asleep. Then he appeared to James, then to all the apostles. Last of all, as to one untimely born, he appeared also to me" (I Cor 15. 3–8). The brevity of his account of what he saw personally may have flowed from the fact that he wrote it primarily to justify his authority as an apostle, but it is also odd that the list of appearances he gave is difficult to reconcile with the rest of the New Testament. There is no other reference in the New Testament to any appearance to James, presumably Jesus' brother who was to fulfill a leading position in the church in Jerusalem after Jesus' death, and it is difficult to see in any of the Gospel stories a reference to any appearance to five hundred people. St Matthew's Gospel refers to Jesus appearing to the eleven disciples and some have suggested that possibly a large number of others were there as well, but there is no definite textual evidence for that. Also, in the Corinthian passage there is no mention of any appearances to the women, nor to any events at the tomb.

That changed with what almost all scholars think was the first Gospel, St Mark's, written in the late sixties some thirty or more years after the events it describes. There is universal scholarly acceptance that it ends with verse 8 of Chapter 16, with verses 9–20 added later by a different hand, although there is debate on whether the original Gospel was intended to end at verse 8. In that final chapter there is the account of three women, Mary Magdalene, Mary the mother of Jesus and Salome going to the tomb and, finding the stone rolled away, they enter the tomb, and "a young man ... in a white robe" tells them that Jesus was risen and that they should tell Peter and the disciples that "he is going before you to Galilee, where you will see him as he told you." The last verse says "And they went out and fled from the tomb; for trembling and astonishment had come upon them; and they said nothing to anyone, for they were afraid." It is perhaps not surprising that some think it was so odd to end a gospel in that way that there must have been a "lost" ending, but at this distance it seems highly unlikely that anyone will ever know for certain.

The next gospels to be written were Matthew and Luke, both probably in the 80s. There is uncertainty as to which came first, although the majority scholarly view is that Luke was written after Matthew. Matthew was writing for a mixed community of Jewish and Gentile Christians while Luke was writing for a predominately Gentile readership. Their accounts of the resurrection, and in Matthew's case some of the details surrounding the crucifixion, are very different.

There is strong evidence from the earlier parts of their Gospels that both Matthew and Luke knew St Mark's Gospel, in some cases not just the stories Mark told but the words used were identical, although both were willing to edit Mark and retell his stories as well. However, some parts of Matthew's Gospel only appear there. In his account of the crucifixion Matthew alone says that "the veil of the Temple was torn in two from top to bottom. And the earth shook, and the rocks were torn apart, and the tombs were opened, and many bodies of the sleeping saints were raised, and going out of the tombs after his resurrection they went into the holy city and appeared to many." No other gospel writer has that story. In his account of the resurrection Matthew follows Mark in telling of the women going to the tomb, but he adds an account of a great earthquake and an angel rolling back the stone and sitting on it. In Matthew's gospel the women do not enter the tomb, but the angel tells them to tell the disciples that Jesus is risen and is going before them to Galilee. Unlike in Mark, Matthew has the women running to tell the disciples, but they then meet the risen Jesus, who repeats the message to tell the disciples to go to Galilee. There follows an account of the guards telling the chief priests what had happened, who suggest that the story should be told that the disciples had stolen the body, and Matthew writes "this story has been spread among the Jews to this day."

In the last four verses of his gospel Matthew tells of the eleven going to the mountain in Galilee. Seeing the risen Jesus, they worshipped him "but some doubted." Jesus then instructs the disciples to "make disciples of all nations, baptizing them in the name of the Father and of the Son and of the Holy Spirit, teaching them to observe all that I have commanded you; and lo, I am with you always, to the close of the age."

Luke follows Mark in the story of the women going to the

tomb, and entering it. In Luke they encounter two men "in dazzling apparel" who ask them "Why do you seek the living among the dead?" The women, who in Luke do not encounter the risen Jesus on their way to the disciples, tell the eleven what had happened "but their words seemed to them an idle tale, and they did not believe them." There then follows the story of the two disciples on the road to Emmaus encountering the risen Jesus although they did not recognize him (Luke 24; vv 13–35). One of them, Cleopas, tells him of the crucifixion and the story of the women going to the tomb and having a vision of angels who told them that Jesus had risen. The risen Jesus, still unrecognized by the two disciples, then proceeds to "interpret to them in all the scriptures the things concerning himself." The two disciples ask the figure to stay with them and as he was at table with them "he took the bread and blessed, and broke it, and gave it to them." They then recognized him and he vanished out of their sight.

They returned to Jerusalem, and joined the disciples, who told them that Jesus had appeared to Simon Peter, and the two told the disciples what had happened on the road, and "how he was known to them in the breaking of the bread." Jesus then appears himself to all the disciples and says "Why are you troubled, and why do questionings rise in your hearts? See my hands and feet that it is I myself; handle me and see: for a spirit does not have flesh and bones as you see I have." He then asks for something to eat and they offer him some fish, which he eats before them. He then explains how this was all to fulfill the scriptures and that they were witnesses of these things. He tells them to "stay in the city, until you are clothed with power from on high." He then leads them to Bethany and there departs from them. St Luke's Gospel concludes "they returned to Jerusalem with great joy, and were continually in the temple blessing God."

The Acts of the Apostles is the sequel to Luke's Gospel and starts with an expanded account of Jesus' departure in the form of the Ascension story. He again told them not to depart from Jerusalem, but "to wait for the promise of the Father" and then, after the ascension, they returned to Jerusalem and elected Matthias, chosen by the casting of lots, to be the twelfth disciple following the departure of Judas Iscariot.

The accounts in St John's Gospel, in the view of most scholars finally written some years after the other Gospels at the earliest about the year 85 CE and possibly later even up to 150 CE, although possibly incorporating some earlier traditions, are also different. There at first only Mary Magdalene goes to the tomb, and finding that the stone had been rolled away ran to tell Simon Peter and the beloved disciple that "they have taken the Lord out of the tomb, and we do not know where they have laid him." Peter and the other disciple ran to the tomb, with Peter going in first and they are reported as seeing the grave clothes lying with "the napkin, which had been on his head, not lying with the linen cloths but rolled up in a place by itself." There follows a slightly odd verse about the beloved disciple entering the tomb "and he saw and believed; for as yet they did not know the scripture, that he must rise from the dead. Then the disciples went back to their homes." It is not quite clear exactly what the beloved disciple believed.

Mary then outside the tomb saw two angels in the tomb, who asked why she was weeping. She explained, and then turned round and "saw Jesus standing, but she did not know that it was Jesus." He also asked her why she was weeping, and she, "supposing him to be the gardener" asked if he had taken the body away, to which the Risen Jesus simply said "Mary" and she recognized him. He said to her "Do not hold me, for I have not yet ascended to the Father" and he then asks her to go to tell the disciples what she had seen, which she does.

According to John on the evening of that day, the first day of the week, i.e. Easter Sunday, the Risen Jesus "came and stood among them" and said to them "Peace be with you." He then showed them his hands and his side, presumably revealing the wounds of the cross. He says again "peace be with you. As the Father has sent me, even so I send you." He then breathed on them, and said to them "Receive the Holy Spirit. If you forgive the sins of any they are forgiven; if you retain the sins of any, they are retained."

John then recounts the story of Thomas, who was not with them on the first Easter Sunday. They told him they had seen Jesus, but he replied "Unless I see in his hands the print of the nails, and place my finger in the mark of the nails, and place my hand in his side, I will not believe." We are then told that eight days later, his disciples were again in the house, and Thomas was with them. Jesus then appeared and said, "Peace be with you." Then he said to Thomas "Place your finger here and see my hands; and put out your hand and lay it in my side; do not be faithless but believing." To which Thomas gives the most comprehensive statement of faith in the whole of the gospels "My Lord and my God!" Jesus then says "Have you believed because you have seen me? Blessed are those who have not seen and yet believe."

Chapter 20 ends with a verse that seems a suitable place to end the whole Gospel, but an additional chapter, which gives an account of Jesus appearing by the Sea of Tiberias, follows it. Many scholars believe this chapter was a later addition although there is no manuscript evidence to support that. Peter and some of the other disciples go fishing, but then they see Jesus on the beach although they do not recognize him. He asks whether they have any fish and they say no. He then advises them to cast their net on the right-hand side of the boat, where they caught so many fish they were not able to haul it in. The beloved disciple says to Peter "It is the Lord." Peter jumps into the sea and the other disciples bring the fish to land, where there is a charcoal fire and they have breakfast. Jesus then asks Peter three times whether he loves him, and when Peter assures him he does,

Jesus commands him to "Feed my lambs," "Tend my sheep" and "Feed my sheep." As Peter had denied Jesus three times earlier in the gospel at the trial of Jesus, this seems fairly clearly to be designed to rehabilitate Peter, but Jesus then foretells Peter's death. Peter then sees the beloved disciple following them and asks Jesus what about him? Jesus' reply "If it is my will that he remain until I come what is that to you? Follow me!" was taken by some to imply that the beloved disciple would not die before Jesus comes again, but that is denied in the text.

This account of the resurrection stories shows that it is very difficult to bring them all together in a single account. It is not just that there are variations in the details of the stories, although they abound. Who and how many went to the tomb and who went in? How many angels – or men in dazzling apparel – were there? What are we to make of the story of the disciples stealing the body of Jesus? But there are also some far more fundamental clashes. Paul said that Jesus was buried, but he has no account of any empty tomb and that must wait until Mark's Gospel was written some fifteen years later. Mark has no account of any appearances by the Risen Jesus, but the other gospels include more and more the later they are written. Matthew has Jesus meeting the women in Jerusalem, but no one else; he has Jesus asking the women to tell the disciples to go to Galilee while the other resurrection appearance in Matthew happens on a mountain in Galilee. In John they occur in Jerusalem and then by the Sea of Tiberias. In Luke the disciples are told to stay in Jerusalem and all the resurrection appearances happen there or nearby.

If Matthew and Luke were written in the 80s, fifty or more years after the first Easter, it is odd that such a fundamental difference between appearances in Galilee (Matthew) and appearances in or near Jerusalem (Luke) remained in them. Then why do the stories become more elaborate the later they appear, perhaps most especially in the latest gospel, St John's? One can understand why Karl Barth, perhaps one of the most influential theologians of the first half of the twentieth century said of them "Unquestionably, the resurrection narratives are contradictory. A coherent history cannot be evolved from them. The appearances to the women and apostles, in Galilee and Jerusalem, which are reported by the Gospels and Paul, cannot be harmonized. It is a chaos. The evangelical theologians of the nineteenth century—my father, for instance—were wrong in trying to arrange things so as to prove the historicity of the resurrection. Their intention deserved praise. But they should have remembered that even the early Church had not tried to harmonize the resurrection stories."

Such differences were long recognized. An eighteenth-century German Enlightenment scholar, Hermann Reimarus, commented on them and thereafter the differences were certainly noted by other scholars, including Albert Schweitzer in his *Quest for the Historical Jesus*. Such discussion continued well into the twentieth century, including debates about whether the tomb was really empty and an exploration of the different accounts of the resurrection appearances. The Church of England's Doctrine Commission chaired by Archbishop William Temple reported in 1938 and said that some members of it believed "the connection made in the New Testament between the emptiness of the tomb and the appearances of the Risen Lord belong rather to the sphere of religious symbolism than to that of historical fact."[2] Other scholars in the last century shared those doubts, including Geoffrey Lampe, Regius Professor of Divinity at Cambridge, the Roman Catholic theologian Hans Kung[3] and Peter Carnley, Archbishop of Perth and Primate of the Australian Church,[4] although others, John Austin Baker, Bishop of Salisbury, for example, came to more conservative conclusions.[5]

More recently three authors have contributed to the debate, all with rather different conclusions. The order in which they were published was John Dominic Crossan,[6] N. T. Wright,[7] and Dale C. Allison.[8]

J. D. Crossan

Crossan is from an Irish Catholic background, but moved to the United States, trained at a Catholic seminary and was ordained a Catholic priest in 1957. He returned to Ireland and became a Doctor of Divinity while at the Irish National Seminary at Maynooth. He then studied in Rome and the Middle East before returning to teach in seminaries in the United States. He resigned his priestly orders and in 1969 joined the staff of DePaul University, a Catholic University in Chicago, and taught there until his retirement in 1995. He has held several prestigious positions in the field of Biblical Research and was co-chairman of the Jesus Seminar, a group of American theologically liberal academics who generally questioned the significance of the apocalyptic element in Jesus' teaching. His *Historical Jesus* was published in 1991, and *Jesus: A Revolutionary Biography* in 1994. Of the three authors considered here, he is the most skeptical about the historical accuracy of the Gospels.

In his prologue to *The Historical Jesus* he notes seven different attempts to understand Jesus against his Jewish background and concludes "Even under the discipline of attempting to envision Jesus against his own proper Jewish background, it seems we have as many pictures as there are exegetes…. That stunning diversity is an academic embarrassment. It is impossible to avoid the suspicion that historical Jesus research is a very safe place to do theology and call it history, to do autobiography and call it biography."[9] This leads him back to examine theory and method. He develops a methodology that includes three levels, anthropology, history and literary. He believes the four Gospel accounts constitute a literary problem. If they are read horizontally, comparing each story with the story as told in another Gospel "It is disagreement rather than agreement that strikes one most forcibly."[10] He concludes that in investigating the sources, the non-Canonical ones must be included as well as the New Testament itself, and that "differences and discrepancies between accounts and versions are not due primarily to vagaries of memory or divergences in emphasis but to quite deliberate theological interpretations of Jesus."[11]

When it comes to his consideration of the traditions about the death and burial of Jesus, he believes the disciples almost certainly fled after the arrest of Jesus and so knew nothing about what happened to Jesus after his arrest other than that he was finally crucified. He doubts that Jesus' followers knew much of the trials, and suspects that the two trials, one before Herod and one before Pilate may well have not happened. "Those twin trials must be emphasized for what they are, namely consummate theological fictions."[12] He also doubts the historicity of the Barabbas incident, which he believes is inconsistent with what is known on other grounds about the brutality of Pilate. He stresses that there was a possible twenty-year gap between the events themselves and Paul writing about them, and a further ten or so years before Mark's Gospel was written. Paul obviously had a particular interpretation of Jesus that will have influenced what he said or how he said it, and the same would be true of each of the Gospel writers. He believed that was quite time enough for various interpretations to be expressed through stories, the historical accuracy of which is debatable.

He notes that the bodies of most people who were crucified were simply left on the cross until their bodies were consumed by wild animals, or possibly buried in shallow graves by the soldiers, which would have led to the same conclusion. He thus doubts the historical accuracy of the tradition of the empty tomb and sees that as all part of a process of several years of creative reflection after the death of Jesus by his followers seeking interpretations of the event. The disciples might well have hoped that Jewish piety might have led to his burial, but they could not have achieved it. "If they had power they were not his friends, if they were his friends, they had no power." Of the story of the burial by Joseph of Arimathea he comments "Need I say that

Mark's naming of him renders him more not less suspect as an historical figure."[13] His conclusion was "With regard to the body of Jesus, by Easter Sunday morning, those who cared did not know where it was, and those who knew did not care."[14]

He wrote:

> What we have now in those detailed passion accounts is not *history remembered* but *prophecy historicized*. And it is necessary to be very clear on what I mean by *prophecy*. I do not mean texts, events, or persons that predicted or foreshadowed the future, that projected themselves *forward* toward a distant fulfillment. I mean such units sought out *backward*, as it were, sought out *after* the events of Jesus' life were already known and his followers declared that texts from the Hebrew Scriptures had been written with him in mind. Prophesy, in this sense, is known after rather than before the fact.[15]

The other distinctive part of his interpretation flows from his use of *The Gospel of Peter*. The existence of such a book was certainly known by the end of the second century as the Church historian Eusebius in his Ecclesiastical History of about 290 CE mentioned it. However, fragments of an actual copy were only discovered in the sands of Egypt in the nineteenth century. It claims to be by Peter himself, but many scholars believe it is pseudepigraphical. There is much discussion about the dating of the book and no one knows for certain. Most scholars conclude it dates from the second century, but Crossan disagrees and believes it predates the gospels and he calls it *The Cross Gospel* although he certainly doubts the historical accuracy of the story and sees it as an early example of the followers of Jesus attempting to find some sort of explanation of what happened. The relevant parts from a translation by Raymond Brown are:

[35] But in the night in which the Lord's day dawned,

when the soldiers were safeguarding it two by two in every watch, there was a loud voice in heaven; [36] and they saw that the heavens were opened and that two males who had much radiance had come down from there and come near the sepulcher. [37] But that stone which had been thrust against the door, having rolled by itself went a distance off the side; and the sepulcher opened, and both the young men entered. [38] And so those soldiers, having seen, awakened the centurion and the elders (for they too were present, safeguarding). [39] And while they were relating what they had seen, again they see three males who have come out from the sepulcher, with the two supporting the other one, and a cross following them, [40] and the head of the two reaching unto heaven, but that of the one being led out by a hand by them going beyond the heavens. [41] And they were hearing a voice from the heavens saying, 'Have you made proclamation to the fallen-asleep?' [42] And an obeisance was heard from the cross, 'Yes.' [43]

And so those people were seeking a common perspective to go off and make these things clear to Pilate; [44] and while they were still considering it through, there appeared again the opened heavens and a certain man having come down and entered into the burial place. [45] Having seen these things, those around the centurion hastened at night before Pilate (having left the sepulcher which they were safeguarding) and described all the things that they indeed had seen, agonizing greatly and saying: 'Truly he was God's Son.'

[46] In answer Pilate said: 'I am clean of the blood of the Son of God, but it was to you that this seemed [the thing to do]. [47] Then all, having come forward, were begging and exhorting him to command the centurion and the soldiers to say to no one what they had seen. [48] 'For,' they said, 'it is better for us to owe the debt of the greatest sin in the sight of God than to fall into the hands of the Jewish people and

be stoned.' [49] And so Pilate ordered the centurion and the soldiers to say nothing.

Crossan believes the notion of the harrowing of hell was a critical part of that Gospel although he believes that was a very Jewish Christian view and the future did not lie with that stream of the tradition. It was steadily marginalized, not least of all by the first Gospel, Mark. He believed that Mark replaced as the overarching model *innocence rescued* to *martyrdom vindicated*. Mark therefore negated the original resurrection account and replaced it with the Transfiguration. The centurion, far from confessing Jesus because of having seen the resurrection as in the Gospel of Peter now does so when he "saw that he thus breathed his last."

Crossan says of Mark, who of course records no resurrection appearances, that for him:

The resurrection was simply the departure of Jesus pending a new immanent return in glory. Between passion and parousia was, for Jesus, the time of absence and non-intervention, and, for the community, the time of waiting in faith and of suffering in imitation. There were no apparitions within that period, and to speak of them after the passion was to invite and commit the same mistake made by the false prophets and false Christs of Mark 13. 5–6 and 13.21–22). Instead, for Mark ... Roman power believed not because of Jesus' apparitions but because of Jesus' exemplary death, and the Transfiguration, a foretaste not of resurrection but of parousia according to 9.9–10, was a rewritten relation of the Cross Gospel's resurrectional apparition back into the earthly life of Jesus.[16]

He also believes that other stories in the synoptic gospels, the feeding of the five thousand with bread and fish, the walking on the water, and the fishing for humans of Mark 1.16–20 and its parallels in Matthew and Luke were post-resurrection stories placed earlier in the Gospels.

The weight of scholarly opinion opposing Crossan's view of the dating of *The Gospel of Peter* certainly makes me doubt that element in his reconstruction, but his broader skepticism about the historical accuracy of the gospels certainly was and still is shared by other scholars within the Jesus Seminar.

N. T. Wright

The second author, N. T. Wright, the former Bishop of Durham, in his *The Resurrection of the Son of God* published in 2003, disputes Crossan's view. He takes a far more conservative line on the history of the gospel accounts and it says much of both him and Crossan that they regularly debate together in America and, while disagreeing, nonetheless appear to respect one another's scholarship.

Wright's book is a massive tome of 738 pages plus notes and he goes into great detail. The first 200 pages are devoted to "Setting the Scene" where he considers attitudes to life after death in ancient paganism, in the Old Testament, and in post-biblical Judaism. He then uses a similar number of pages to consider resurrection in Paul's writings, and then a similar amount of space on resurrection in early Christianity apart from that in Paul. It is not until page 585 that he starts to consider the Easter stories themselves, and then for the final fifty pages of the book considers belief, event and meaning. He states firmly his conviction that the emergence of the belief that Jesus was raised from the dead could only have happened if the tomb was indeed empty and the resurrection appearances actually happened.[17]

The essential point in his thesis relates to what he calls "second Temple Judaism." After Solomon's Temple was destroyed by the Babylonians in 586 BCE it was rebuilt by Zerubbabel and then later overhauled and refurbished by Herod the Great, and finally completed twenty years or so before Jesus' birth. It was the Temple known to Jesus and it continued until the destruction of Jerusalem in 70 CE by a Roman army. Wright maintains that from the building of the original second Temple a view of resurrection developed in Judaism that he describes as belief in "life *after* life after death." That is to say when someone died they went to the place of the departed and waited there until there would be a final resurrection which would be the undoing or defeat of death at the end of time. Jesus' resurrection was therefore seen as the first example of what would be the final stage for everyone.

Against that background he interprets all that was said about resurrection in the New Testament, and believes on that basis it is possible to show the overall theological consistency and historical accuracy of the New Testament accounts of Jesus' resurrection. He recognizes that each of the authors had their own particular way of telling the story, but believes there was an overarching historical consistency behind what was said even though some details in the various accounts were different. On that basis he argues for the broad historical accuracy of all of the New Testament accounts.

Many people confronted by the sheer weight of scholarship he brings to the exercise simply accept his argument, and the book has been influential in Britain and America. However, there are some major problems about his thesis.

First, was the view of resurrection in second Temple Judaism as consistent as he suggests? One of the first reviewers of the book was James Dunn, Lightfoot Professor of Theology at Durham University, where Wright had just arrived as Bishop having completed his book in his previous time as a Canon of Westminster. Dunn asks:

Has Wright argued too strongly for a uniform belief in resurrection as life after life-after-death?... Has he read a single coherent story out of material that is much more diverse and fragmentary?... Has he assumed that there was such a uniform version of Jewish and Christian hope for life beyond death and read the often diverse and fragmentary data to conform with that version?... Such questions are particularly pertinent since Jesus himself is recalled as likening resurrection to angelic existence in heaven (Mark 12.25).... Is it so clear from this episode that Jesus' answer depended on the unspoken corollary, that if the patriarchs still exist then they will certainly be raised to life after life-after-death? Or is the more obvious deduction from the passage that Jesus envisaged resurrection life as the angel-like existence already enjoyed by the patriarchs? Alternatively put, has Wright tried too hard to squeeze what was a diverse hope, 'fleshed out' in different ways, into a single uniform mould?[18]

Secondly, is the historical accuracy of the stories as obvious as he suggests? James Crossley of the University of Sheffield reviewed Wright's book in the *Journal for the Study of the Historical Jesus* and says of Wright's dislike of any assumption that Jewish writers rewrote history:

> when discussing a dispute between the Roman Emperor and Gamaliel II's daughter, he can say it is 'no doubt fictitious.' Most would agree. But this degree of suspicion is never applied to the story of the resurrection, the empty tomb, and all the other strange accompanying stories, stories that for many people are much more unlikely than a rabbi's daughter meeting an emperor. If we are to take stories on a case-by-case basis, why is it that pagan and Jewish texts can be deemed fictitious but Christian stories, including the obviously secondary Mt. 27.51–53, are not? If we are going to take Christianity seriously in its Jewish and pagan contexts then we must expect the Gospel writers to make up stories just as Jews and pagans did. Historically speaking it

is extremely unlikely that the Christians behind the Gospel traditions were immune to this standard practice.[19]

Crossley's reference to Matt. 27: 51–53 refers to one of the more remarkable statements in Matthew's account of the crucifixion mentioned earlier. "The earth shook, and the rocks were split; the tombs also were opened, and many bodies of the saints who had fallen asleep were raised, and coming out of the tombs after his resurrection they went into the holy city and appeared to many." Wright says it is impossible to adjudicate on the question of historicity and that the account remains a puzzle, "but it is better to remain puzzled than to settle for either a difficult argument for historicity or a cheap and cheerful rationalistic dismissal of the possibility. Some stories are so odd they may just have happened." By contrast, John Fenton in his Pelican Commentary on St Matthew's Gospel unhesitatingly describes it as "legendary."[20]

But that is only one example of Wright's more conservative view. Possibly more significant is his acceptance as historical of the account of Jesus appearing to St Thomas in John 20. According to that Gospel it happened a week after the first Easter in the presence of many of the disciples. If that is historically the case then it is very odd that it was first mentioned in a Gospel that was finally written towards the end of the first century or maybe even later and neither St Paul nor any of the other Gospel writers mention it. Did they not know of it or did they not think it important? It seems much more likely that this was a story the author of the fourth gospel included for theological rather than for historical reasons.

Thirdly, why should we accept the second Temple view of eschatology, even if it was as consistent as Wright implies, as the only correct one now? Wright describes this view and assumes it to be the basis for Christian hope now, not just in his major work on the resurrection but also in a subsequent book, *Surprised by*

Hope.[21] Exactly what second Temple Judaism believed is difficult to ascertain, especially in a culture then that was not so obsessed with evidence for facts as a post-Enlightenment world became. It is at least possible that then some would have thought the first few chapters of Genesis were correct history rather than myth, and, if they thought about it at all, at that time they may have thought the earth was flat. Subsequent discoveries have shown them to be wrong about the past and their present so why should we believe they were correct about the future? On many issues our knowledge and understanding has developed from earlier times and humanity has not always found it difficult to change its view, even if changing it took some time.

Fourthly, lying behind his thesis is Wright's almost visceral dislike of the Enlightenment.[22] He seems to assume that those who do not share his view of the literal truth and accuracy of the New Testament accounts only do so because they have succumbed to "Enlightenment thinking." However, the Enlightenment was not a consistent and unified program but rather a wide intellectual movement with many themes. No doubt in some parts there were elements of arrogance, which is what Wright says he most objects to in it, but arrogance is scarcely the preserve of any one movement. The Enlightenment built on and subsequently contributed to the scientific method that led to some major discoveries and in that process stressed the value of reason over faith and careful investigation over theological dogmatism. If one thinks of the way the Roman Catholic Church originally treated Galileo, it is possible to conclude that arrogance there lay not in scientific method but in the Church's conviction that it possessed and guarded the truth. The Enlightenment also stressed the need for tolerance and freedom of conscience, which might well seem a better way of living than the religious wars that so disfigured the centuries that preceded it.

Two historians of the Enlightenment, John Robertson[23] and Anthony Kenny,[24] both stress that while there was opposition to religious superstition not all Enlightenment thinkers were opposed to religion. Anthony Kenny, who is certainly not ignorant of Christian theology having trained as a young man as a Catholic priest before becoming a very noted historian of philosophy, observed that the Roman Catholic Church was very late in recognizing the value of critical biblical study, and concluded his chapter on the religious legacy of the Enlightenment "Nowadays it is not in Rome or in Canterbury that one finds the early chapters of Genesis taken literally, but in the fundamentalist evangelical churches that have proliferated, especially in the United States. In such communities it is common to speak with some disdain of 'the enlightenment project'. But within traditional, mainstream Christian communities, the Enlightenment can fairly claim to have made many of its points."[25] While Wright certainly does not claim that the early chapters of Genesis were historically correct he does make similarly dismissive statements about the overall thrust of the Enlightenment, surprisingly so for an Anglican bishop.

Fifthly, what if "resurrection" is a metaphor? Wright writes "The terms 'literal' and 'metaphorical' refer, properly, to *the ways words refer to things,* not to the things to which the words refer. For the latter task, the appropriate words might be 'concrete' and 'abstract'"[26] However, James Dunn at the end of his review mentioned earlier wrote:

Another major concern is whether Wright's treatment of resurrection as metaphor helps or hinders his thesis. If 'resurrection' can be used to denote return from exile (itself a metaphor?), for overthrow of the current political system, and also for a new quality of life already experienced by the baptized Christian, should we regard all these usages as part of a single 'language game'? Or has the term itself become a metaphor whose validity does not necessarily depend on there being a future referent? When the term can be used of physical resuscitation (Matt. 11:15's reference to Isa. 26:19–20), of experience of life now, and disaggregated into a 'first' and 'second resurrection' (Rev 20:5), why should it be so self-evident that the hope of final resurrection is not another variation on the metaphor? None of this is to say that Wright is necessarily wrong in deriving a uniform thesis from such diverse evidence – though I suspect he would have been fairer to the evidence if he allowed that the hope entertained was not quite so uniform.[27]

Certainly, many in the twentieth century considered resurrection as a metaphor, although Wright obviously does consider it as "concrete." But that he considers it so does not remove the question Dunn raises.

Dale Allison in his review of Wright's book comments: "Wright's passionate belief in the traditional Christian confession was not the result of his historical researches but rather an article of faith that has informed his scholarly work from its inception."[28] That is certainly the impression his book gives; he had decided in principle what he wanted to say before he had put pen to paper and seeks to almost bludgeon his readers into submission. That is why I do not find his overall argument convincing.

However, at one point I certainly do agree with Wright. In *Surprised by Hope* he talks about the consequences of the resurrection for the way Christian people live now. He says that if Christianity is not just about "going to heaven when we die" but living life now with the conviction that the resurrection tradition points to something about the final victory of Jesus then it is the task of the church to make that real in the world we know now. Among the many examples he gives is dealing with the huge imbalance that international debt gives to poorer nations, which he rightly sees as an affront to fundamental Christian values.[29] So while I disagree with him about the detailed interpretation of the gospel accounts and about the notion of life after death or even life after life after death, on the consequences of living that out in today's world whether that be about international debt or the other practical issues he raises, I completely agree with him on the consequences of resurrection belief. But it seems to me that can be built on a metaphorical use of the notion of resurrection as well as on the more literalistic, or as he would put it, concrete conclusions of his overall thesis about historicity.

Dale C. Allison

Allison is an ordained elder in the Presbyterian tradition and was Professor of New Testament Exegesis and Early Christianity at Pittsburgh Theological Seminary when he wrote his book on the resurrection. He is now Professor of New Testament Studies at Princeton Theological Seminary. He was on the Editorial Board of *The Journal for the Study of the Historical Jesus*. He takes a different view from Crossan and the Jesus Seminar on the apocalyptic element in Jesus' teaching, and on a number of Crossan's other arguments, but he also takes a different approach to Wright on the evidence for the resurrection. It is well described in his *Resurrecting Jesus*, which has the advantage over Wright's book in only being 375 pages long! It contains six essays on matters about the historical Jesus and the last and longest one gives the book its title. It was published in 2005 and so was able to take full account of Wright's book.

He outlines seven explanations or interpretations of the resurrection given in the past and of these possibilities he says he would personally prefer to believe in the literal resurrection and explains why, but he acknowledges areas of personal doubt about that conclusion. The first comes from what one author Will Herberg describes as all "the literalistic pseudo-biological fantasies" traditionally associated with belief in the resurrection[30] and he combines that with "the necessary discontinuity between Jesus' bodily resurrection and the proposed resurrection of the rest of us." He explains also what he believes about personal life after death and expands that in another more recent book *Night Comes, Imagination and the Last Things*. I will discuss both in a later chapter.

He then considers the formulas, confessions and appearance stories in the New Testament and says the view that "God raised Jesus from the dead" was evident even from some of the earliest of Paul's letters. In I Corinthians 15, Paul also talks about "the third day" and that phrase is then used quite often in the various Gospels, all of which were written after Paul's letters. He notes a number of possible explanations of that and concludes "As these are all good possibilities, the most we can infer with any confidence is that Christians found three-day language appropriate because they believed that very little time elapsed between Jesus' crucifixion and God's vindication of him. There is some reason to suppose the Gospels correct when they represent Easter faith as emerging very soon, indeed within a week, after the crucifixion."[31] However, in his examination of the various accounts of the appearances of Jesus recorded in the Gospels and Acts he concludes "they do not, upon initial analysis, take us much beyond 1 Corinthians 15:3–8. For we simply cannot, using our historical-critical tools, determine to what extent the particulars in the accounts preserve old or authentic memory; our instruments are too blunt for such fine work. Even if there are certain recurring themes and motifs, we cannot without further ado equate those with historical events."[32]

He notes that some of the accounts of appearances were to more than one person and that leads to what I find the most fascinating part of his book. He believes it is problematic to assert "because of their multiple witnesses and shared nature (they are) without real analogy. There are, on the contrary, many first-hand accounts of several people seeing at once the apparition of a person recently deceased. There are likewise innumerable accounts of various people seeing an apparition over an extended period of time ... the truth of the matter, welcome or not, is that the literature on visions of the dead is full of parallels to the stories we find in the Gospels."[33]

The Society for Psychical Research undertook in 1882 a survey of so-called paranormal experiences and that work continued for some years, but Allison says that they were all eclipsed when a British medical doctor, Dewi Rees, reported on a research project into the experience of the death of married partners in the *British Medical Journal* in 1971. "Rees discovered that, of the 293 widows and widowers he interviewed, fully 47% of them believed that they had come into close contact with their dead spouse. Most of those encounters took place not long after death, but there were also occurrences many years later. A fair percentage of those encounters were fully fledged apparitions."[34] He goes on to note that such contact is not confined to surviving partners or those in mourning. "All parts of the general public report a high incidence – surveys from Western Europe and North America vary anywhere from about 10–40 percent – of apparent contact with the dead through dreams, voices, felt presences, as well as visions while wide awake. Those experiences are, moreover, often experienced as quite vivid and real.... Another result of some interest is that religious faith or belief in an afterlife is not a necessary prerequisite of these experiences."[35] He comments that while one might consider them "the hallucinatory projections of self-deceived mourners ... the first point for historians of the New Testament is that the sorts of experiences just encountered are common, and they typically seem quite real to the participants.... Although many will be sure to resist compiling parallels between what we find in the Gospels and what we find among the bereaved generally, it is simply not true that the events in the Gospels are utterly without analogy."[36]

He is surely right when he asserts "the post-mortem manifestations of an unremarkable husband to his isolated widow is not going to generate the same significance as the reappearance of a messianic figure whose followers are living within an eschatological scenario that features the resurrection of the dead. Context begets meaning."[37] However, he summarizes his approach to stories of post-mortem experiences:

> They have their place once we embrace a methodological pluralism, which in this connection means attempting to sort out and then explain data to the best of our abilities from different points of view and within different interpretative frameworks. No one method or set of comparative materials will give us all the answers we seek. We strive rather to learn what we can from each method or set, in the knowledge that each may help us with some part of the picture we are trying to piece together. So in the present case I eschew explaining the appearances of Jesus in terms of typical appearances of the dead – an unfeasible task anyway given our limited knowledge and understanding of apparitions in general – but simply ask what light a wider human phenomenon might shed on some of the issues surrounding the resurrection traditions.[38]

He then examines whether a vision might be veridical of an objective external truth or a subjective creation of the person having the vision. He notes that "no human experience can be independent of thoroughly psychological and neurochemical mechanisms."[39] Of the argument that appearances shared by a collection of people make that less likely he notes that "there are examples of collective hallucinations in which people claimed to have seen the same thing but, when closely interviewed, disagreed on the details … how do we know that the Twelve, subjected to a critical cross-examination and interviewed in isolation, would have all told the same story? Or would their testimony rather have been riddled with inconsistencies. No one will ever know."[40] He notes, though, that "skepticism runs both ways. If the data are too meager for the apologist's needs, they equally do not suffice for the rationalistic antagonists of the church ... we have restricted access to the past, some things are intractable, and this may well be one of them."[41]

On the matter of the empty tomb Allison gives seven reasons for doubting it and seven for thinking it historical. He summarizes the argument "Looking back over the debate regarding the empty tomb, there is no iron logic on either side. There is a decent case for it, and there is a respectable case against it. Both sides, moreover, have their faults and suffer from a scarcity of proof: neither exorcises all our doubts."[42] He comes down on the side of thinking it more likely than not that the tomb was empty, but with caution. "A judgment in favor of the empty tomb, which will for ever be haunted by legendary stories of disappearing and raised bodies, must remain, if accepted, tentative."[43] He writes, though, that a vacated tomb does not, it hardly needs underlining, tell us why this all happened. We have here rather an historical dead end. It is always possible to imagine that someone, for reasons unknown, removed the body, as Mary Magdalene first supposed in John 20:13–15. Later,[44] in an *Excursus*, he discusses the possibility of burial by Joseph of Arimathea and gives his reasons for believing that tradition might be historically accurate, in opposition to Crossan's view.[45] The impression that is most clearly given by his work on the empty tomb and the burial by Josephus of Arimathea and indeed the book as a whole is of a scholar seeking to balance carefully the evidence rather that trying to force the reader to adopt one side or the other.

In the final section of the main part of his book he recognizes that the historical data are ambiguous and how they are read probably depends on the individual reader's presuppositions. "The truth one discerns behind the texts is largely determined by desires, expectations, and religious and philosophical convictions already to hand. We cannot eschew ourselves."[46]

Conclusion

After considering the work of three major and internationally recognized Christian scholars all considering the same basic textual evidence from the New Testament and non-canonical sources, we cannot fail to notice that they come to very different conclusions. I take that to be as much a comment on the original material as on the individual authors. It is impossible to be certain about what happened to cause resurrection belief.

As I also personally believe it is impossible to be certain about the notion of life after death, I suppose that is not surprising. I suspect Crossan, who apparently shares my doubts about life after death, is nonetheless too skeptical of the New Testament evidence, but that Wright is too ready to accept its historical accuracy. I therefore find Allison's cautious view more congenial, although as a later chapter will show, I question his approach to life after death. There is no way of avoiding uncertainty in this life!

	All	Christian	Non-Christian	No Religion	Active Christian
Believe	44%	72%	35%	9%	93%
Happened word-for-word as in the Bible	17%	31%	14%	1%	57%
The Bible has some content that should not be taken literally	26%	41%	21%	8%	36%
Do not believe in the resurrection	50%	23%	56%	88%	5%
Don't know	6%	5%	9%	3%	2%

In that connection it is interesting to observe the results of a ComRes survey commissioned by the BBC on attitudes to the resurrection in the UK conducted prior to Easter 2017. They interviewed 2010 individuals of whom 1019 described themselves as Christian, 177 non-Christian, 752 of no religion and 315 Active Christian. They were asked about their overall belief in the resurrection and then four options to choose from.

Personally, I am in the 41% of Christians who do not believe that all the biblical stories should be taken literally.

The next stage of this inquiry notes more recent thought about the very notion of life after death, including some from outside the church. A consideration of secular thought must sit alongside the Christian tradition if we are honestly to face all the issues.

Chapter 3 Endnotes

1   Richards HJ. *The First Easter: What Really Happened?* Fount Paperbacks; 1980 provides an excellent review of the material from a Roman Catholic scholar.

2   Church of England Doctrine Commission. *Doctrine in the Church of England.* London: SPCK. 1938. p. 86.

3   Kung H. *On Being a Christian.* Glasgow: Collins Fount Paperback; 1978. pp. 343–81.

4   Carnley P. *The Structure of Resurrection Belief.* Oxford: Clarendon; 1987.

5   Baker JA. *The Faith of a Christian.* London: Darton, Longman and Todd; 1996. An Appendix gives his view on the resurrection narratives.

6   Crossan, JD. *The Historical Jesus: The Life of a Mediterranean Jewish Peasant.* Edinburgh: T & T Clark; 1994. *Jesus; A Revolutionary Biography.* New York: HarperCollins; 2010.

7   Wright NT. *The Resurrection of the Son of God.* Minneapolis: Fortress Press; 2003.

8   Allison DC. *Resurrecting Jesus.* London and New York: T & T Clark; 2005.

9   Crossan JD. *The Historical Jesus.* p. xxvii.

10 p. xxx.

11 p. xxx.

12 p. 390.

13 p. 393.

14 p. 394.

15 Crossan JD. *Jesus: A Revolutionary Biography.* p. 163.

16 Crossan JD. *The Historical Jesus: The Life of a Mediterranean Peasant*

17 his arguments are summarized in pages 686–696.

18 *Journal of Theological Studies.* Vol 55: October 2004. p. 630.

19 *Journal for the Study of the Historical Jesus* article by James Crossley. June 2005.

20 Wright NT. *The Resurrection of the Son of God.* p. 636. Fenton, J C. *The Gospel of St Matthew.* Penguin Books; 1963. p. 444.
21 Wright T. *Surprised by Hope.* SPCK; 2007.
22 Wright NT. *The Resurrection of the Son of God.* p. 712f gives a summary of his view.
23 Robertson J. *The Enlightenment.* OUP; 2015.
24 Kenny A. *The Enlightenment.* SPCK; 2017.
25 p. 109.
26 Preface p. xix.
27 *Journal of Theological Studies.* Vol 55: October 2004. p. 630.
28 Allison D. Introductory editorial. *Journal for the Study of the Historical Jesus.* June 2005.
29 *Surprised by Hope.* pp. 228–9.
30 *Resurrecting Jesus.* p. 219.
31 p. 232.
32 p. 269.
33 p. 269f.
34 p. 273.
35 pp. 274–275.
36 p. 277.
37 p. 284.
38 p. 285.
39 p. 295.
40 p. 297.
41 p. 298.
42 p. 331.
43 p. 332.
44 p. 334. Allison gives possible explanations in the rest of that and the following paragraph.
45 pp. 352–363.
46 p. 343.

Chapter 4

Modern Secular Developments

In the twentieth century there have been significant examinations of the notion of life after death from a more or less secular point of view. Some were critical, others more ambiguous. In this chapter I shall consider four of those books, but first I believe one of the most significant developments was from the combined criticism of two philosophers.

The Decline of Cartesian Dualism

In Chapter 2 I described the dualism that René Descartes advocated. His theory came under sustained attack in a book published in 1949 by the then Waynflete Professor of Metaphysical Philosophy at Oxford, Gilbert Ryle. He summarized what he described as "the official doctrine," "Mind and body are normally harnessed together, but after the death of the body the mind may continue to exist and function." He suggested that in this "official doctrine," bodies are in space and so are publicly observable, but minds are essentially private. "A person has two histories, one consisting of what happens to his body, the other consisting of what happens in his mind. The first is public, the second private. The events in the first history are events in the physical world; those in the second are events in the mental world.... One person has no direct access of any sort to the events of the inner life of another."[1]

He continued in a robust combative style:

Such in outline is the official theory. I shall often speak of it, with deliberate abusiveness, as 'the dogma of the Ghost in the Machine.' I hope to prove that it is entirely false, and false not in detail but in principle. It's a category-mistake. It represents

79

the facts of mental life as if they belonged to one logical type or category ... when they actually belong to another. The dogma is therefore a philosopher's myth.[2] I am saying that the phrase 'there occur mental processes' does not mean the same sort of thing as 'there occur physical processes', and, therefore, that it makes no sense to conjoin or disjoin the two.... The belief that there is polar opposition between Mind and Matter is the belief that they are terms of the same logical type.[3] Mind and body both exist but they indicate two different senses of 'exist', somewhat as 'rising' has different senses in 'the tide is rising', 'hopes are rising', and 'the average age of death is rising.' I shall try to prove that the official theory rests on a batch of category-mistakes by showing that logically absurd corollaries flow from it. The exhibition of these absurdities will have the constructive effect of bringing out part of the correct logic of mental-conduct concepts.[4]

Ryle then examines a number of notions, the distinction between knowing how and knowing that,[5] the will,[6] emotion,[7] ending with self-knowledge[8] and the result was a book that certainly called into question Cartesian dualism and which led many to abandon it.

His conclusions were reinforced when Wittgenstein's Philosophical Investigations were published after Wittgenstein's death in 1951. His thought had been widely discussed in philosophical circles prior to his death and indeed some thought Ryle might have got some of his own ideas from those unpublished thoughts. Wittgenstein's views flowed from his approach to language; in order to think we need a language in which we can express our ideas. He therefore questioned whether the notion of a "private world of mind" could exist without a public language in which it was expressed.

Anthony Kenny's book *The Metaphysics of Mind* was partly a tribute to Ryle, but also in some areas modified Ryle's conclusions.

"I came to realize that the ideas that were expressed with crudity as well as vivacity by Ryle were developed more painfully and more subtly by the much greater genius of Wittgenstein."[9]

Ryle's views were sometimes described as "behaviorist," where all behavior is seen to be a response to external environmental forces and not to mental processes at all. Kenny commented: "Fortunately, dualism and behaviorism do not exhaust the alternatives open to the student of the philosophy of mind. The most significant philosopher of mind in the twentieth century was Ludwig Wittgenstein. He thought both dualists and behaviorists were victims of confusion. His own stance was a middle position between the two. Mental events and states, he believed, were neither reducible to their bodily expressions (as the behaviorists have argued) nor totally separable from them (as the dualists had concluded). Even when we think our most private and spiritual thoughts, he argued, we do so through the medium of a language that is essentially tied to its public and bodily expression. Unlike the behaviorists, Wittgenstein did not deny the possibility of secret and spiritual thoughts; but on the other hand, he demonstrated the incoherence of the Cartesian dichotomy of mind and body."

Cartesian dualism is not widely accepted now in philosophy although a few philosophers still sympathize with it. Anthony Kenny noted that "among educated people in the West who are not philosophers it is still the most widespread view of mind. Most contemporary philosophers would disown Cartesian dualism but even those who explicitly renounce it are often profoundly influenced by it."[10] Reasons for that will be examined in Chapter 5.

Kenny also commented on the question of "soul." Some might say that to have a soul is no more than to say that we have a mind. Others might imply more than that, that there is an immortal soul. He commented "I merely want to make the great difference between this controversial claim that human beings have souls and the truism that human beings have minds.... If, according to Cartesian dualism, consciousness is purely the content of the private world of introspection, then it is philosophical nonsense. For if 'consciousness' is the name for something that can only be observed by introspection, then the meaning ... must be learnt by a private and uncheckable performance. But a word only has a meaning as part of language; and language is essentially something public and shared,...The criteria by which the investigator judges that certain mental events are taking place, or certain intellectual abilities are lacking, are the normal behavioral ones; what the patient says and does, or fails to be able to say and do."[11]

As an expert in Thomism, Kenny's additional comment should be noted.

> I do not ... wish to take issue with those who believe in disembodied immortal souls. For what I have just said would not necessarily be rejected by those who believe in such souls. We may take Thomas Aquinas as a spokesman for such believers. Aquinas undoubtedly believed that each human being had an immortal soul, which could survive the death of the body and continue to will and think in the period before the eventual resurrection of the body to which he looked forward. Nonetheless, Aquinas did not believe he could survive, as the person he was, in a self that was distinct from the body, because he did not think disembodied souls were persons. Even after death, he believed his soul was the soul it was only because it was the soul of a particular body. Fully personal survival, according to him, was only possible if there was to be a resurrection of the body.[12]

However, it is noteworthy that later Kenny wrote "while I am agnostic about the existence of God, I am not agnostic about life after death: I am sure that belief in it is an illusion."[13]

Later Developments

Over the years since Ryle and Wittgenstein wrote there have been many publications about Life after Death. Some have come from people who have had a strong personal experience, often but not exclusively of a near-death experience, that have convinced them of the reality of life after death. Those experiences and alternative explanations of them are discussed in the next chapter. But four books, each taking a slightly different line from the others, two largely in favor of some notion of life after death and two far more critical, are worthy of note. The first partly believes in the notion, the second does not and the final two, published in successive years, are considered in the same order, pro and anti.

Life After Death by Arnold Toynbee, Arthur Koestler and others

Published in 1976,[14] the two main authors were academically distinguished and their views would have commanded respect. Toynbee wrote the first chapter "Man's concern with Life after Death." He thought there was no doubt about what happens to the body after death, it disintegrates. Some believe they have seen ghosts, but a ghost that did not appear in human form would be invisible. He commented "an unembodied live human being has never been seen, except on the hypothesis that a ghost is alive but is incorporeal. This hypothesis is unconvincing. It seems more likely that the apparent visibility of a ghost is an hallucination." However, he also wrote "Material media such as sight, sound, and touch are not the only possible means of communication between conscious personalities, and it is conceivable that, in some cases, the appearance of a ghost may be an incidental accompaniment of a real, non-visual communication between the person who sees the ghost and another person who may either be dead or else still incarnate but not physically present."[15] A later chapter by Rosalind Heywood, a well-known parapsychologist expanded on that in ways he found convincing. "There is now a widespread recognition of the reality of extrasensory perception as a medium of communication between two or more incarnate persons. Evidence for its reality is, to my mind, cogent." However, he also observed "extrasensory communication between the living is contested; and the reality of extrasensory communications with the dead, or with conscious personalities that have never been incarnate, is disputed even more vehemently. The wise course for inquirers into the destiny of a personality after death is surely to keep their minds open for entertaining the possibility that in some cases the dead may have indicated the reality of the survival of their personalities by really entering into communication with persons who are still incarnate."[16] That was, of course, strongly disputed by others.

Toynbee then surveys a series of beliefs, or non-beliefs, in some sort of life beyond death, including in the Buddhist tradition. He noted views from belief in some form of reincarnation to belief that death was the end of the human personality; which view an individual held depended upon how he viewed religion. He thought the majority then (in 1975) adhered to one or other of the historic regional religions, but for others that was only nominal; "in their heart of hearts they now believe that, at death, the personality is extinguished; and the number of frank believers in extinction is growing." The decline was a recent event: Even in the Western world, disbelief continued to be exceptional until the second half of the nineteenth century of the Christian Era. Till that date, a majority of Western men and women continued to believe in "the resurrection of the body and the life everlasting." But since 1914 he thought western civilization has been in disarray. However, he also noted the potentially positive effects of belief in life after death. "A belief in the permanent survival of a human personality after death also reinforces a person's innate sense of responsibility for his conduct during his terrestrial lifetime, if the belief in survival is accompanied by a belief in a post-mortem judgment.... belief in the post-mortem immortality of a human personality gives consolation to someone who has been bereaved of the companionship on earth of a fellow human being whom he loves. The anguish of bereavement is mitigated by the assurance that the parting which is inflicted by death is only temporary."[17] He observed that belief was not as widespread as it had been "In the year AD 1975 an increasing number of Westerners are living in a spiritual vacuum. The discomfort and dismay of these present-day heirs of the Western civilization goes far towards accounting for the crisis by which the Western world is now being beset."[18]

Toynbee says "At the present day the belief in a re-embodiment of the dead is still officially obligatory for all Zoroastrians, Jews, Christians, Muslims, Hindus and Buddhists; and these six religions, between them, command the adherence of a great majority of mankind."[19] "If experiences at this level are considered with an open mind, they throw flickers of light on the unverifiable possibility of life after death which has been man's concern ever since the unknown date at which our ancestors awoke to consciousness."[20]

A chapter on Primitive Societies by Cottie A. Burland concluded "A belief in an after-life seems to be endemic among the human race."[21] Others wrote chapters on other religions, although there were some surprising omissions in the details. The discussion of Ancient Greek ideas only dwelt on those who believed various things about the continuation of "the soul," but there was no discussion of those Ancient Greeks who doubted such things such as Epicurus or even Cebes, the friend of Socrates quoted by Plato.

Ulrich Simon, then a Professor and later Dean of King's College, London, contributed a chapter "Resurrection in a Post-Religious age." He hears his editor asking "Tell us what happens to me, I cannot tell. I refuse to regard myself in isolation, for in isolation, out of context, I am not only lost, but I want to be lost. Who would want to live on in the emptiness of self?"[22] He believed Glory was a concept that has been abused for centuries and concludes by thinking that music is the one medium that gives a clue. "Without music, polyphonous in fugal richness, the claim to glory cannot be substantiated. Therefore no adult Christian (pity the truly deaf whose hope must be deferred) can claim to have access to this glory without singing and playing, and listening to, the *Glorias* of our liturgies. There, and there only, are incarnate the strains of eternal glory, which mediates the depth of dying and the height of living. The secular age will recover its belief not through theological words but through the trumpets of the *Gloria*."[23]

Rosalind Heywood was the well-known parapsychologist and psychic who was Vice-President of the Society for Psychical Research. The Society did valuable work in its early period in investigating various claims, many of which it showed to be spurious. However, in its later life there were major criticisms, even from members of the Society. Eric Dingwall resigned and wrote "After sixty years' experience and personal acquaintance with most of the leading parapsychologists of that period, I do not think I could name half a dozen whom I could call objective students who honestly wished to discover the truth. The great majority wanted to prove something or other: They wanted the phenomena into which they were inquiring to serve some purpose in supporting preconceived theories of their own."[24]

In Rosalind Heywood's own chapter, she outlines the personal experiences she interpreted through Extra Sensory Perception. It is notable that the Wikipedia article on her includes a number of scholarly criticisms of her methodology and in an article in the *New Scientist*, John Cohen wrote that although she was "entirely convinced" from the results of card-guessing experiments "Heywood fails to detect the vulnerability of these studies ... she has failed to see the shortcomings of the experimental procedure itself." Cohen wrote the objection to Heywood's psychical claims is that no adequate evidence had been presented. That article was published in 1959, some years before Toynbee wrote. It is therefore surprising that Toynbee placed so much confidence in her work. While in his chapter he recognizes that many of the world's religions had accepted arguments for life after death and recognized that such belief could provide comfort to the bereaved, it is also surprising for someone with his reputation as a scholar of ideas that he made no reference to criticisms of Cartesian dualism when he advances notions that seem to be dependent on it.

The final chapter was by Arthur Koestler. He spoke of the spilt between reason and emotion which is endemic to the human condition. "Emotion is the older and more powerful partner in the divided household, and whenever there is conflict, the reasoning half of the brain is compelled to provide spurious rationalizations for the senior partner's urges and whims.... The old brain which occupies that larger part of our skulls passionately rejects the notion of personal non-existence ... accordingly the old brain considers survival as self-evident."[25] I suspect today that would be disputed.

He then wrote about what he describes as "de-materialized matter" and compared that change in thinking about the material world as related to what we think about mind. In the process he made what some might see as a rather generous assessment of parapsychological phenomena. "The point to retain is that phenomena which half a century ago seemed to defy the laws of nature now appear less offensive because those laws are no longer regarded as strictly valid; and the weird theories advanced to account for those phenomena now appear less preposterous because the theories advanced by physicists are even more weird and insulting to naïve common sense.... An object flying through the air without physical cause, as often reported in Poltergeist phenomena, is no longer considered to offend the laws of nature, only the laws of probability."[26]

Koestler describes "the trend towards a new conception of holism, expressed in the Mach principle, which states that the inertial properties of terrestrial matter are determined by the total mass of the universe about us."[27] Bertrand Russell flippantly remarked that it "savors of astrology." However, a fifteenth-century Platonist wrote "Firstly there is unity of things whereby each thing is at one with itself. Secondly there is the unity whereby one creature is united with the others and all parts of the world constitute one world."[28] Koestler maintains the majority of contemporary physicists would underwrite these lines. Schrodinger was one such physicist and philosopher and he concluded that the consequence of what we know about particle physics led to "only one alternative, namely the unification of minds and consciousness. Their multiplicity is only apparent, in truth there is only one mind."[29]

Koestler noted that Sherrington and Penfield propounded a modified Cartesian dualism of brain and mind, where mind was the controlling agency. He comments "If we reject both naïve materialism and rigid Cartesian dualism, the principle of complementarity offers a more promising approach."[30] He therefore held to the possibility that "individual consciousness is a kind of holographic fragment of cosmic consciousness – a fragment temporarily attaching itself to a body with its filtering and computing apparatus and eventually returning to, and dissolving in, the all-pervading mind-stuff. About the first process we know a little: about the second nothing at all. But the first may contain some clues to the second."[31]

He concluded:

this outlook, however subjective and vague, is at least sufficiently definite to exclude belief in personal immortality – warts and all. At the same time the hypothesis of a cosmic psi-field is not more fantastic than the physicist's superspace replete with quantum foam, and even has some affinities with it. Carrying speculation one last step further, we might assume that the cosmic mind-stuff evolves as the material universe evolves, and that it contains some form of historical record of the creative achievement of intelligent life not only on this planet, but of others as well.[32]

Such a view is, of course, highly speculative and would probably not be widely accepted today. What is clear from *Life After Death* is that there were a variety of views amongst its distinguished contributors, not all of which were consistent with one another. It was a significant but dated contribution to a complex debate.

Immortality: The Quest to Live Forever and How it Drives Civilisation[33]

Stephen Cave was a philosopher, then a diplomat and is now a full-time author; his book was published in 2012. He examines four paths to immortality, all of which have had positive benefits but none of which he concludes is viable today. The first he entitles staying alive, which motive has certainly driven much positive medical research that has made lives better, "But the science that promises to take us still further also has other lessons: that the processes of aging and decay are deeply embedded in our bodies; that the very technologies that could help us could also prove our destruction; and the world we live in will not tolerate human life for ever.... This narrative is both seductive and productive, but it will not deliver on its promise."[34]

His second path is resurrection. His particular concern is not to seek to explain the resurrection of Jesus, but to consider the very notion of the resurrection of anyone. How can the various atoms that once comprised our bodies be brought back together in any way that can sustain the notion that it is our resurrected body? He notes difficulties that have long preoccupied some theologians, the first of which he calls the Cannibal Problem.

Atoms that were once part of us may well become part of someone else, and he notes the estimate that 98% of the particles that form us are replaced every year. If we are resurrected, what happens to those particles that were part of us but are now part of someone else? He concludes "Despite two thousand years of trying, the Cannibal Problem remains without solution."[35]

He calls his second resurrection problem the Transformation Problem. We clearly change over the years and look different. What is resurrected? "The resurrectionists have therefore run into a contradiction: on the one hand your survival depends on exactly the same atoms being reassembled just as they were before you died; yet on the other hand, the post resurrection you is supposed to be a different creature altogether, made of invincible stuff and arranged so differently that you no longer require even a metabolism ... this sounds more like replacement than resurrection."[36]

He calls his third resurrection problem the Duplication Problem. Are you resurrected as you were when you were five years old or as your adult version? "The reassembled five-year old would have as much claim to be you as the reassembled adult version. He concludes "these three problems show that even God would have great difficulty in physically putting you back together on Judgment Day in a way that would mean it was really *you* rising from the grave."[37]

On the basis of that and a further chapter looking at Mary Shelley's novel Frankenstein as another form of resurrection which turned out to produce a monster he concluded "All versions of the Resurrection Narrative start out by accepting that we really do die and decay. But it is very difficult to make sense of how someone can return from this kind of utter extinction.... Resurrection is alone in taking death on the chin – and this is the problem; most philosophers believe that if something has completely ceased to exist – like a person who has died and rotted, or a painting that has been burned – then any new version that is made, however similar, is nothing more than a copy."[38] That leads to his third path, the notion of the immortality of the soul.

The replacement of resurrection by the immortality of the soul certainly removed the problems of resurrection, and Cave concludes that it became a powerful alternative because it allowed the idea of a continued existence after death of the essential being of a person, i.e. the soul. The most powerful romantic picture is Dante's Divine Comedy, where the image of the soul of the dead Beatrice ascending to heaven provided medieval Christendom with an alternative picture to resurrection, which had a popular appeal even if it did not satisfy theological purists. It retains its adherents even to this day, with Cave maintaining 71% of Americans believe in the soul, and 60% of the United Kingdom and Germany believing in it. However, he holds it is a fatally flawed view, shown in particular by the evidence that physical damage to the mind and brain are the source of dramatic changes to people's personalities and characters. He believes that demonstrates the complete physical connection of the mind and body with personality. "Everything the soul was supposed to explain – thoughts, consciousness, life itself – has been shown to be dependent on the body. We therefore have every reason to believe that all these faculties – from memory to emotion to the most basic forms of awareness – cease when the body ceases. There is simply nothing left over for the soul. As a hypothesis, it is redundant."[39]

He describes his fourth path as legacy; people hope through their lives to have created a legacy either of achievement or financial wealth that will give them a sort of immortality. He gives a number of examples, Alexander the Great, probably the most successful military commander ever although often demonstrating extraordinary ruthlessness nonetheless died at the age of thirty-two. His fame lasts to today but does that form of legacy really mean existing? He quotes one of the noblemen who fought at Troy "Death in ten thousand forms hangs ever over our heads, and no man can elude him; therefore let us go forward and win glory." Cave comments "His message is clear; if there was some way of achieving eternal youth or cheating death then he would gladly take it. But there isn't."[40]

But what of children? Albert Einstein wrote "Our death is not an end if we can live on in our children."[41] No doubt the genetic inheritance we pass to our children will be passed on by them to their children, so to that extent we participate in a continuance of life well beyond our own death, but "there is a stumbling block to taking the claims of biological immortality literally: consciousness…. It may be true that it is therefore a mistake to think that 'I' am really born and really die, as 'I' am actually part of a broader continuum. But: this phase that is me gives every impression of having a distinct individual consciousness; and when that phase is over, that consciousness disappears…. I might live on in the great web of life, but if not consciously, then that claim to immortality rings a little hollow."[42]

He concludes with a number of observations on the consequences of his views, all of which personally I find wise.

First, "if this life here on earth is regarded merely as a series of tests for a place in another life then it is necessarily devalued: with eyes fixed firmly on their future bliss, the immortalist fails to grasp the value of being *now*." As the French philosopher, Albert Camus wrote, "if there is a sin against this life, it consists perhaps not so much in despairing of life as in hoping for another life and in eluding the implacable grandeur of this life."[43]He notes an obsession with personal survival fosters a profound selfishness and also comments on the psychological effects of eternity: "There are as I see it two sets of problems: on the one hand, the boredom and apathy that would result from having done and seen everything there is to do – that is from having already lived a very long time; and on the other hand, the paralysis that would result from having an infinite future in which to do any further things. Both these problems, the backward looking and the forward looking, threaten to suck the meaning out of life and leave one wishing for a terminal deadline."[44]

Secondly, he comments on the strength of the Wisdom Literature, where any belief in immortality was certainly not central. Psalm 90 advised its readers "Teach us to number our days that we may get to the heart of wisdom." Epicurus wrote around 300 BCE: "For all good and evil lies in sensation and death is the end of all sensation." "While we are, death is not: when death comes, we are not. Death is thus no concern either to the living or to the dead. For it is not with the living, and the dead do not exist." Cave noted also Wittgenstein's comment "death is not an event in life, we do not live to experience death" and Woody Allen's comment "I am not afraid of death, I just don't want to be there when it happens." Cave comments "He can rest assured; he won't be…. The conscious experiences we have had *are* the totality of our lives: death, like birth, is just a term that defines the bounds of those experiences, like the frame of a painting that serves to delineate and accentuate the image within."[45]

Thirdly, he notes the need for gratitude. "Awareness of self might be important, but excessive concern with the self only exacerbates the fear of death, or loss of self, and leads one to a life of self-absorption. In order to combat this, we should cultivate selflessness or identifying with others. Similarly, picturing the future helps us to plan a successful life, but excessive concern with the future causes us to focus on the tribulations that lie ahead of us – and we forget to live now. Therefore we should learn to live more in the present moment. And third, imagining all the things that could threaten our existence might help us to avoid them, but in excess it leads us only to worry about what we might lose rather than appreciate what we have. Therefore we should cultivate gratitude."[46] "The very faculties that make you aware of death also enable you to live, experience the sublime, appreciate art, connect with other people and with nature, to build and create and understand. Modern science has if anything taught us that these facts – of life and mind – are even more extraordinary than our ancestors might have thought. And what these facts suggest is that before we rue our plight of a short life overshadowed by death, we should be grateful – very, very grateful – that we have a short life at all, and with a brain capable of appreciating and creating so much wonder."[47] He notes the comment of Robert Emmons, "gratitude is positively related to such critical outcomes as life satisfaction, vitality, happiness, self-esteem, optimism, hope, empathy, and the willingness to provide emotional and tangible support for other people, whereas being ungrateful is related to anxiety, depression, envy, materialism, and loneliness." It is no coincidence that gratitude is one of the common themes through the world's wisdom literature and a powerful antidote to the fear of death. As the Greek Stoic Epictetus put it: "He is a wise man who does not grieve for the things which he has not, but rejoices for those which he has."[48]

Then on a number of very practical matters he notes Roy Baumeister's recommendation on identifying with others: "The most effective solution to this threat (of death) is to place one's life in some context that will outlast the self. If one's efforts are devoted to goals and values that project many generations into the future, then death does not undermine them."[49]

On focusing on the present, "happiness is only to be found in the present moment, as only the present moment is real. The past is gone; the future mere speculation. If you are happy now, then you are happy always, as there is only now. But equally if you spend each moment worrying about your future happiness, then happiness will always elude you, and your life will be one of anxiety. And, as we have seen, worrying about death – something we can never experience – is the most foolish worry of all."[50]

By way of summary, two of his final comments are:

The fact is, we have not evolved to be carefree and joyful: we have evolved to perpetuate ourselves – at the expense of everything else, including our happiness. The immortality narratives only fuel this striving and its underlying causes. Although these narratives might sometimes succeed in assuaging our existential angst, they are not otherwise a recipe for contentment. The Wisdom Narrative is different: instead of dismissing existential anxiety by denying death, it attacks the underlying attitudes that might make us think we ought to be afraid of death in the first place. By doing so, it aims to cultivate an appreciation of this life and this world, as it is, right now.[51]

A civilization of those who face up to their mortality is therefore one worth striving for. Indeed, combining this with the rest of the Wisdom Narrative, we could even boldly claim that awareness of mortality offers the best of all possible situations; knowing that this life will have an end puts a limit on our time and so makes it valuable. The fact of mortality imparts to our existence an urgency and allows us to give it shape and meaning – we have reason to get up in the morning and engage with the world while we can: we have reason to make this the best of all worlds, because we know there is no other. Yet that which sets the limit – death – is not something we can ever suffer from or in any way experience. As essentially living things, we cannot even literally be dead. All we can know is life; and by accepting that it is finite, we can also know to treasure it.[52]

Afterlife: A History of Life after Death[53]
Philip Almond is Emeritus Professor of Religion at the University of Queensland and states in the prologue to his book:

We do not know what follows our deaths, any more than we know what preceded our lives. Hence, this book is about our imaginings of the afterlife from the ancient Greeks and Hebrews to the present. For all we know, one, some or none of these imaginings may be true. But whatever the case, the history of the afterlife is the history of our hopes that there will be something after death and of our fears that there will be nothing. And, granted that there is something rather than nothing, it speaks to our dreams of eternal happiness, to our nightmares of eternal punishment, and of the myriad ways in which these have been inflected over the centuries.

He speaks of the two foundational narratives within Western thought about the afterlife. One is a narrative built around the anticipation that our lives will continue immediately after the death of each of us. The soul will be weighed in the balance, judged and sent to the bliss of heaven or cast into the pit of hell. The other narrative is driven by the expectation that our eternal destinies will be finally determined not at the time of death, but at the time when history ends, when this world will be no more and when Christ returns to judge both the living and the dead. There will then only be two possible destinations for our souls reunited with our bodies; to enter an eternity of bliss or be thrown with the damned into the everlasting fire. He wrote "Within the first few centuries of the Christian era, the history of the afterlife in the West became the history of a constantly fluid series of negotiations, contestations and compromises between the two versions of our futures beyond death ... modern histories of the afterlife in the West have focused on one or other of those narratives. This book, by contrast, is shaped by the interplay, tensions and conflicts between them within a history that tells the story of each of them."[54]

He examines the Old Testament notions of death. The commandment in Deuteronomy shows that consulting ghosts or spirits was abhorrent to the law of Israel, but that did not stop it happening as in the case of Saul consulting the Witch of Endor. Sheol was seen as the place of the departed, a place for a very shadowy existence, which had elements of being a place of punishment. It was similar to the Hades of Classical Greece. Surprisingly, Almond says little about the Sadducees, who were the guardians of the Temple. They provided the High Priest of Judaism and definitely rejected any notion of life after death. He points out, however, that in the Old Testament as a whole there was no clear and uniform picture of what happened to the dead. Rewards and punishments developed as it was seen that any afterlife might be the place for righting the injustices of this world, and in time that developed into the notion of some sort of division among the dead, although there were conflicting views on whether that happened immediately after death or at the end of time.

Most of his book is devoted to examining the developing, and sometimes very changing, view of Christianity, and therefore more properly belonged to Chapter 2 of this book looking at Christian views. Visions of Hell and Purgatory preoccupy much of the account. However, he notes that by the time of the seventeenth century some thinkers concluded that the extinction of life at the moment of death was a more comforting prospect than eternal punishment in the fires of hell, or even a temporary punishment followed by extinction. "Such plebeian materialism was often combined with a pantheism that found the divine in everything."[55]

He notes, however, that by the turn of the twentieth century, Darwinian agnosticism was to segue, in the face of scientific materialism, into philosophical certainty. However, in contrast to materialist certainties, Kant's questioning mind played a key role in twentieth-century liberal theology's reluctance to say much at all about the afterlife. The search for the meaning of life was replaced by the quest for meaning in life. As we shall see in Chapter 6, the Roman Catholic theologian Karl Rahner distinguished between eternity defined as a succession of moments extending into an infinite future and an eternity outside time. According to Rahner, the dead have only the latter form of eternity. "Eternity is not an immeasurably long-lasting mode of pure time, but a mode of the sprit and freedom which are fulfilled in time.... When we open our hearts to the silent calm of God himself, in which they (the dead) live; not by calling them back (like the spiritualists) to where we are, but by descending into the silent eternity of our own hearts, and through faith in the risen Lord, creating in time the eternity which they have brought forth for ever."[56] Almond comments "In twentieth-century Protestant and Catholic theology, at least on the liberal side, the afterlife had become an afterthought." The modern afterlife is, however, not always a matter of individual immortality, but on occasion one of final absorption into the divine (or the recognition that the self and the divine are one). Aldous Huxley popularized what he called "the perennial philosophy," where truth is manifested in many forms, but it flows from a single fountain. The essence of each individual soul was equivalent to the essence of the universe (Gog): "the Atman, or immanent eternal Self is one with Brahman, the Absolute Principle of all existence and the last end of every human being is to discover this fact for himself, to find out Who he really is." This followed a nineteenth-century Hindu tradition of Swami Vivekananda ... in this tradition the mystical experience of personal identity with God in this life foreshadows the liberation of the individual at death from individual consciousness.

Almond concludes by discussing the disenchantment of the world flowing from science, and therefore spoke of a need for a re-enchantment. Enchanted worlds now sit alongside a disenchanted one. Tolkien, C. S. Lewis's Narnia and Harry Potter all give examples. He ends his survey:

the gap between this life and the next is more opaque. More generally, the distinction between an enchanted and a disenchanted world is harder to sustain intellectually. The enchanted imagination lives alongside disenchanted reason. The spaces between here and eternity, now and then, fact and fiction, the literal and the metaphorical, the religious and the magical, the rational and the imaginary are blurred. The modern world is one of multiple meanings, both enchanted and disenchanted. We can inhabit both an enchanted and a disenchanted world, a secular and a sacred history, this realm and the next, as a matter of leisure, or pleasure, or utmost seriousness. Belief can be embraced and disbelief happily and willingly suspended.[5]

Whether that applies to a particular individual probably depends on their personality. Personally, I find it difficult to suspend disbelief.

Almond's view is not, however, the view of the last book in this chapter to be considered.

The Myth of the Afterlife: The Case against Life after Death[55]

This book was published in 2015 and according to its editors there is no other collection on life after death that has covered such a wide range of issues. What unites some thirty authors, most of whom hold or have held major academic posts in philosophy, psychology, psychiatry or neuroscience, is the view that biological death permanently ends a person's experiences.

In a foreword, Steve Stewart-Williams, then Senior Lecturer in psychology at Swansea, looks at reasons why beliefs in any afterlife developed and discusses four that are often suggested. First wishful thinking, which he thinks contains a grain of truth but some problems; does such belief really provide comfort when, in some cases like belief in hell, it provides no comfort at all? Secondly, social glue, which was at least partly provided in some societies because it encouraged good behavior and discouraged the opposite. Thirdly, social control, which functions for the benefit of those who promote the belief, although he notes some religious beliefs also function to liberate people rather than shackle them. Fourth, primitive science might have pointed to various phenomena, dreams for example, and thought the explanation might have been an afterlife. But if that is the explanation then why does it continue on when evidence points the other way?

He then examines two other explanations that come from evolutionary science. First, belief can be seen as a spandrel that works, for example, at one stage it piggy-backed on a particular theory of mind that suggested it was distinct from the body. This was certainly a partial explanation at one stage in history. Secondly there is Richard Dawkins' notion of a "meme," or unit of culture. It stays alive because it continues to circulate in a culture. This memetic approach does not displace the other views but provides an overarching framework which Stewart-Williams finds convincing. The meme only needs to be advantageous to itself.

Finally, he asks why pursue the question. Might it be best to leave people with their comforting thoughts? He suggests four reasons why this should be opposed. First, because truth matters as an end in itself. Second, because afterlife beliefs are certainly not always comforting. Third, because clearing away a superstitious belief ushers in a more accurate view of the world, and this view is beautiful in a rather stark kind of way. Fourth, there is a moral obligation to confront the true nature of death.

The editors then describe with some precision what they mean by life after death, that "we irrevocably lose consciousness, once and for all, at the end of life." One of the editors Keith Augustine is even more specific: "the starting point of the volume is the extinction hypothesis. It only concerns itself with *personal* survival. Impersonal forms of 'survival,' such as the notion that *thought* in general will persist beyond the obliteration of one's own consciousness, or that the erasure of one's distinct personality will coincide with its absorption into an eternal 'cosmic mind' are not our concerns here." He notes two principle kinds of eternal life prevalent in Western theological literature, the immortality of the soul, or the mysterious resurrection of the body, and he notes also the Eastern conception of rebirth, that the soul enters another body.

There are four parts to the book.

Part I. Empirical Arguments for Annihilation

The mind is dependent on the body. In Chapter 2 Matt McCormick, Professor of Philosophy at California State University presents a case for thinking most mental functions are dependent on brain activity, which does not sit well with any sort of soul that can function independently of the brain. Jean Mercer is Professor Emerita of Psychology at the Richard Stockton College of New Jersey. She compares the view that personality traits are determined by the soul with the view that they are a consequence of biological factors and concludes that biological factors, which include genetic factors and temperamental factors alone can account for them. David Weisman is a neurologist and examines progressive neurological diseases and their effect on brain decline and the decline of consciousness. He concludes that when intact and functional brain tissue required for one's consciousness and personality becomes dysfunctional and dies, everything traditionally characterized as distinctive of the soul dies with it. A philosopher and neurobiologist also look at the evidence of brain damage and examine it in the context of the two options of dualism and materialism. They conclude that only the latter is consistent with the evidence that when brain activity ceases so does consciousness. Further chapters from other neuroscientists and philosophers argue that the relationship of neural structures is the root of consciousness. The mind is dependent on a functioning brain.

As will be noted in the next chapter of this book there is a major debate in neuroscience about exactly what is the relationship of the human being to the brain, but very few would assert that the mind could survive without a functioning brain. Opposition to this point of view comes from some Christian theologians, which will be examined in Chapter 6, but also from parapsychology, where Keith Augustine comments "Out of sheer intellectual honesty a few brave souls within parapsychology have conceded the daunting challenge that this evidence poses for survival. But their only apparent recourse is to argue – quite implausibly – that the ambiguous parapsychological evidence for survival actually outweighs the virtually incontestable neuroscientific and other evidence for extinction." "The aim of part 1 is to present the full force of this evidence and its devastating implications for survival, noting crucial inadequacies in the existing responses of survivalists to the challenges posed by neuroscience, behavioral genetics, and evolutionary psychology."[59]

Part II. Conceptual and Empirical Difficulties for Survival

"Even those who believe in Life after Death often have great difficulty imagining just what post-mortem existence would be like. Presuming that you could survive death, without a biological body, in what form would you persist." "Several contributors to Part II argue that there are fundamental difficulties confronting attempts to provide concrete answers to these sorts of questions, difficulties which arise from the incoherence or infeasibility of surviving death in particular ways."[60] In his Introduction in chapter 1, Keith Augustine considers three options, the first being a disembodied mind. He comments "Without eyes with which to see, ears with which to hear, or indeed any sense organs at all, how could a *bodiless* mind perceive its environment?"[61] How somebody with a disembodied afterlife could ever be identified is an intellectual challenge that has not yet been met. His second option is the notion of an astral body. But how can we provide any positive characterization of astral minds? Our inability to detect astral bodies or ethereal bodies is problematic. Susan Blackmore considers those questions and concludes that none of these possibilities can adequately solve the problems they generate. His third option is bodily resurrection. Chapter 3 of this book considered that issue as it applies to the resurrection of Jesus, but in the more general sense of resurrection there are two possibilities, reassembly or replication. Both face insurmountable difficulties. At some point a human being is going to share all his atoms with another human being in a way that makes resurrecting everybody impossible. This makes reassembly impossible to believe, so most of the literature is on whether a replica would really be the same as the person who died. Personal identity requires us asking what makes a person at any moment the same as some past or future person. Keith Augustine comments "It may be logically possible for us to survive death in some substantial sense if God chooses to resurrect us through replication or reassembly, (but) the mere fact that an idea is not self-contradictory is hardly grounds for thinking it is true. Of the three ways of surviving death that I have just outlined, resurrection is the least likely route to be realised."[62] Theodore Drange also considers the possibility of some form of bodily resurrection and concludes that it is conceptually impossible. "The main idea behind this argument is that such an afterlife would conceptually require that a person be a kind of thing that could be rendered plural. But since persons are not that type of thing, such an afterlife is not conceptually possible."[63] Also, while we know a good deal of how brains work, it is very difficult to understand any way a non-physical soul could influence brains. Even if God could create a mental and physical replica of you, it could never be identical to you.

Part III Problematic Models of the Afterlife

In the introduction Keith Augustine offers arguments against the internal coherence of predominately theological conceptions of the afterlife, in particular the ideas of heaven and hell. The notion that the inhabitants of heaven could be ecstatic in the full knowledge that some of their loved ones are trapped in a state of permanent anguish contravenes a number of fundamental moral principles. "The reward of eternal bliss far exceeds what is merited by any finite good done during an individual's lifetime. A case can also be made that some of the suffering of this world is so horrific that nothing could adequately compensate for it." But also the punishment should fit the crime. Unending torment far exceeds what is merited for any finite evil done."[64] He also considers the problem of moral luck, some people are virtuous because of their fortunate background and others are not virtuous because of their terrible background. "Considerations about moral luck suggest that a single human lifetime rarely, if ever, affords individuals with sufficient opportunities to be tested to determine what sort of fate they really deserve."[65] There is also some evidence to suggest moral failings can be a consequence of neurophysiological causes. Also, to the argument that facing suffering produces moral character, he states "Earthly life is dominated by ample instances of apparently pointless harms that are not offset by any potential moral benefits for anybody.... If a final afterlife state can be perfect in the complete absence of suffering, there is no morally sufficient reason to subject individuals to the ills of earthly life to begin with."[66]

In Chapter 20 of Part III, "Problems with Heaven," Michael Martin suggests three criticisms of the idea of heaven; that it lacks coherence, that it is difficult to reconcile it with standard defenses against the argument from evil such as the free will defense, and that it is unfair and thus in conflict with the goodness of God. He asks if those in heaven have free will; if they do not then is it really heaven, but if they do, what happens if they "fall"?

He also points out that heaven is sometimes considered simply God's gift to those who believe, and in other forms a reward for good behavior. In the case of the former given the evidence for belief is at the least ambiguous why should those who genuinely do not believe in that way be punished for a legitimate doubt? In the case of those for whom it is a reward for good behavior, what are the criteria for deciding good behavior? The biblical picture of God's behavior is that it is sometimes cruel and arbitrary. Do those who follow that get accepted into heaven but those who doubt or question it get punished? Heaven seems very unfair!

Raymond Bradley, an Emeritus Professor of Philosophy from Canada, believes that the very notion of Hell as a place of permanent punishment is untenable, because ultimately if God is the creator, he is responsible for evil as well as good. If people are evil it is because God allowed them to be so. He also believes that the biblical pictures of hell are so ghastly that it is difficult to see how so-called evil acts could merit such eternal punishment.

In his Introduction Keith Augustine also notes the Eastern view of rebirth and the notion of karma. "Moral development presumes that we can learn from our mistakes and become more virtuous as a result of what we have learned. But in each new incarnation, the memories of previous lives are either totally obliterated or completely inaccessible, and so no such trial and error learning can actually take place over multiple lifetimes.... Without continuity of memory from one lifetime to the next, karmic justice amounts to rewarding or punishing one person for another person's deeds."[67] Ingrid Smythe, a freelance writer, also argues against the notions of karma and rebirth.[68] She suggests that karma explains how bad things happen to apparently good people, but there is no evidence at all that receiving good or bad things is a consequence of our moral status. Bad things happen to good people, and good things happen to bad people, any hidden "moral" explanation for that is very hidden! Evil in the world cannot be explained by karma, there is much evil that occurs for other reasons, natural disasters, for example. If karma asserts that there is no unjust suffering in the world then it is wrong. Similarly there is no evidence for the rebirth doctrine.

Part IV Dubious Evidence for Survival

The other principal sources of belief in an afterlife are reports of paranormal phenomena said to signify human post-mortem survival. The types of survival evidence covered include reports of apparitions of the dead, hauntings, and poltergeists; out-of-body and near-death experiences; of spontaneous past-life memories; and of mediumistic communications with the dead. Yet it is quite possible to interpret many of these as hallucinations, and when a supposed apparition was seen by a number of people "One paradoxical finding of early psychical research was that apparitions perceived by more than one person, some of those present and in a position to see the apparition often reported seeing nothing at all. And even when apparitions are collectively perceived, there are often substantive discrepancies between the reported observations of different witnesses. The simplest explanation for this kind of differential perception is social contagion: one person sees an ambiguously human form and then primes others present to 'see' the same thing."[69] On Out of Body Experiences he notes some characteristics of them which suggests that "OBEs are abnormal models of reality that draw upon memory and imagination when the brain is under stress or when sense input is disrupted."[70] And the traits often found in NDEs suggest they are "hallucinations brought on by expectations of immanent death or medical crisis."[71] Of those who claim to remember experiences of their past lives he concludes "The most obvious possibility is that parents living in a society where reincarnation is widely accepted have coached their children to tell tales of remembering the former life of another family's deceased relative, who is often of a higher caste, in order to obtain better living conditions for their children."[72]

On the matter of mediums he gives a good deal of evidence for suggesting most of them are fraudulent, either deliberately or unconsciously.

Keith Augustine's conclusion is "I would like to see the afterlife debate move forward, beyond armchair plausibility arguments and closer to a scientific consensus (one way or the other) built upon unequivocal data. If the survival question is ever going to be answered decisively, it will only be answered through direct scientific investigation."[73]

Public opinion

I should not end this chapter without noting what public opinion polls indicate about the range of beliefs. In America about 75% of the population believes in some form of life after death and that has remained fairly constant over a number of years. In the United Kingdom the figure is far lower. According to the ComRes study of religious beliefs quoted at the end of Chapter 3 carried out for the BBC in 2017, 46% of the population believes in it and 46% does not. Men are more doubtful than women, 36% believe and 56% do not, but those figures are almost exactly reversed for women. The same survey broke down responses according to religious belief. Of those who described themselves as Christian, 61% believed in it and 31% did not. A further break down to those who described themselves as "active Christians" said 85% of active Christians did believe in it, but 11% said they did not and 4% said they did not know.

Conclusion

The books considered in this chapter show that there has been a considerable debate well beyond the bounds of any traditional religion about the very notion of life after death. In the world of philosophy the near collapse of Cartesian dualism as summarized by Anthony Kenny is very significant for much Christian thought and Wittgenstein's comments on the nature of eternity have also had a profound effect. I have found it an illuminating experience to encounter the other books, and personally, if I had to choose, my sympathies most of all would lie with Stephen Cave's book. He shows some very clear problems with the very idea of immortality in any form itself, yet does so while not totally dismissing any sympathy for religion as shown in his positive approach to Wisdom literature.

In Chapter 6 I shall examine what has happened in the Christian Church in response to such challenges, but first I must consider in the next chapter one matter that features a great deal in the literature on the afterlife, Near Death Experiences. In doing so I have encountered a major issue about the world of neuroscience, which also has its implications for any future Christian thought.

Chapter 4 Endnotes

1   Ryle G. *The Concept of Mind*. Penguin Books; 1949. pp. 15–16.
2   ibid p. 17.
3   ibid p. 23.
4   ibid p. 24.
5   ibid Chapter 2.
6   ibid Chapter 3.
7   ibid Chapter 4.
8   ibid Chapter 6.
9   Kenny A. *The Metaphysics of Mind*. Clarendon Press; 1989. Preface p. v.
10 *ibid* p. 2.
11 ibid pp. 18, 22,30.
12 ibid p. 31.
13 Kenny A. *Brief Encounters: Notes from a Philosopher's Diary*. SPCK; 2018. p. 45.
14 Toynbee A, Koestler A. *Life After Death*. Weidenfeld & Nicholson; 1969.
15 p. 4.
16 p. 5.
17 p. 20.
18 p. 20.
19 p. 29.
20 p. 36.
21 p. 53.
22 p. 152.
23 p. 153.
24 Article by Eric Dingwall in Kurz P. *A Sceptic's Handbook of Parapsychology*. Prometheus Books; 1985. pp. 161–174.
25 p. 239.
26 p. 246.
27 p. 246.
28 p. 247.

29 p. 250.

30 p. 254.

31 p. 255.

32 p. 258.

33 Cave S. *Immortality*. Biteback Publishing; 2012.

34 *Immortality*. p. 87.

35 ibid p. 144.

36 ibid p. 115.

37 ibid p. 116.

38 ibid p. 144f.

39 ibid p. 209.

40 ibid p. 220.

41 ibid p. 246.

42 ibid p. 254f.

43 ibid p. 280. Camus A. Summer in Algiers. In: *The Myth of Sisyphus, and Other Essays*. Hamish Hamilton; 1955.

44 ibid p. 282.

45 p. 295.

46 p. 296.

47 p. 302.

48 p. 303.

49 p. 299.

50 p. 300.

51 p. 304.

52 p. 306f.

53 Almond PC. *Afterlife: A History of Life after Death*. London, New York: I B Taurus; 2016.

54 p. 2f.

55 p. 99.

56 p. 179f.

57 p. 190f.

58 Martin M, Augustine K. (eds) *The Myth of the Afterlife: The Case against Life after Death*. Lanham, London: Rowman & Littlefield; 2015.

59   p. 5.

60   p. 293f.

61   p. 6.

62   p. 10.

63   p. 295.

64   p. 12.

65   p. 13.

66   p. 15.

67   p. 18f.

68   Chapter 22.

69   p. 21.

70   p. 22.

71   p. 23.

72   p. 25.

73   p. 32.

Chapter 5

Near Death Experiences and Neuroscience

Accounts of the experiences of some of those who have been close to death have been recorded for many years. Dr Sam Parnia, a medical doctor in a Southampton Hospital while a Research Fellow at Southampton University, noted some early examples in his book *What Happens When We Die?* The first recorded example is from the fourth century BCE in Plato's *Republic*, where an ordinary soldier, after a near fatal injury on the battlefield, "is revived in the funeral parlor and describes a journey from darkness to light accompanied by guides, a moment of judgment, feelings of peace and joy, and visions of extraordinary beauty and happiness." Similar experiences have happened to some other people in such circumstances, including in some cases a sort of rapid "life review" when people's whole lives seem to flash before their eyes. Parnia describes the experience of a British Admiral who narrowly escaped drowning in Portsmouth Harbour in 1795, which appeared to include such a life review as described in a local newspaper at the time.[1] Such experiences have been recorded in different cultures and although many of the features are common these cultures are reflected in the descriptions; when people saw religious figures "Where they were specifically identified, they were always described according to the person's religious beliefs; no Hindu reported seeing Jesus, and no Christian a Hindu deity."[2]

In 1975 the psychiatrist Raymond Moody coined the term "near-death experiences" (NDEs), which title is used in much of the recent research. Among the many difficulties of assessing them is that many occur unexpectedly, after an accident when someone falls from a great height or nearly drowns, or when someone is seriously ill in hospital, for example, after a stroke or heart attack. If anyone medically qualified is near them at the time they are likely to put all their energy into seeking to save life rather than asking complex questions about the patient's experiences at the time. Also not everyone in near-death conditions has such experiences, so any sort of careful comparison under measurable clinical conditions is difficult if not impossible. But that has not stopped interest in the subject by some in the medical field.

In 1983 Bruce Greyson, Professor Emeritus of Psychiatry and Neurobehavioral Sciences at the University of Virginia, produced the Greyson Scale, measuring whether the account of a particular experience counted as an NDE. He identified sixteen different items noted by some of those who have had such an experience:

1. Experiencing an altered state of time
2. Experiencing accelerated thought processes
3. Life Review
4. Sense of sudden understanding
5. Feelings of peace
6. Feelings of joy
7. Feelings of cosmic oneness
8. Seeing/feeling surrounded by light
9. Having vivid sensations
10. Extrasensory perception
11. Experiencing visions
12. Experiencing a sense of being out of a physical body
13. Experiencing a sense of an "otherworldly" environment
14. Experiencing a sense of a mystical entity
15. Experiencing a sense of deceased/religious figures
16. Experiencing a sense of a barrier or point of no return.

The scale gives to each of those features a score of 0, 1 or 2 depending on the judgment of each person who had the NDE.

The potential maximum score is 32 but Greyson identified as an NDE any score above 7 as not all of the items occur in every case. The patient can normally recall the experiences vividly and they have often led to significant and normally positive changes in their lives.

NDEs have been subject to careful analysis by neurologists such as Peter Fenwick of the Maudsley Hospital, who analyzed over 300 examples,[3] and Dr Parnia. Both of them advocated further research into NDEs and Paul Badham, until recently Professor of Theology at Lampeter takes them as possible evidence of life after death.[4] Both Fenwick and Badham co-operated in supervising a PhD on NDEs by Penny Sartori, an intensive care nurse, so they are academically acknowledged experts in this field, and Sartori's thesis was published.[5] Badham notes in his foreword to her book that it is particularly of interest in that it examines some near-death experiences that are less positive than those normally quoted.

Part of the background to understanding the whole matter is that there have been significant changes in how to define the moment of death over the last fifty or sixty years. Clinical death used to be defined as when the patient stopped breathing, but since the advent of resuscitation, when people who have stopped breathing have been enabled to recover, the moment of death has been moved to when brain death occurs. In most cases it makes little difference, stopping breathing indicates death is imminent for the vast majority of people, but there are some examples of people recovering from that point and apparently experiencing no long-term brain damage. That might especially, but not exclusively, apply when a person's body temperature has been lowered, for example, by starting to drown in cold water. It does seem that while loss of breathing meaning that no blood flows to the brain might cause some brain damage, the brain might nonetheless continue to function for some time, even hours if the body temperature lowers sufficiently. Parnia's particular expertise is in resuscitating those who have suffered from a cardiac arrest, where he thinks brain activity can continue for up to 30 minutes. The fact of these experiences is not doubted, but interpretations of them vary. Parnia suggests three broad interpretations. The first category is theories that seek to show how they are generated by neurological effects of what is happening in the brain at the time. A second set of theories is psychological rather than neurological. "NDEs could be an unconscious defense mechanism in which an individual separates themselves from specific activities or emotions in order to avoid their reality."[6] He concludes that while this remains an interesting theory that maybe explains some elements of NDEs, it has not been tested. His third set of theories is inevitably more contentious in the wider medical community namely transcendental theories. "It has been suggested that an NDE might be a spiritual experience indicating the existence of a soul and providing a glimpse into the afterlife, as had in fact been claimed by the vast majority of those who had experienced it."

There is no doubt that many who have experienced NDEs are convinced of the transcendental explanation. Many have written books on the subject and they are certainly the reasons some give for believing in life after death. However, to understand these interpretations it is necessary first to consider developments in neuroscience.

Neuroscience

The twentieth century saw great advances in neuroscience, which have certainly had their effect on many people's views about life after death. However, alongside that whole development there has been a significant debate within neuroscience itself about its philosophical basis. This is well represented in *Philosophical Foundations of Neuroscience* by M. R. Bennett, a distinguished neuroscientist himself, and P. M. S. Hacker, a philosopher. It is a major work of some 450 pages and it is only possible here to consider a few of their major themes.

> If we are to understand the neural structures and dynamics that make perception, thought, memory, emotion and intentional behavior possible, clarity about these concepts and categories is essential.... Both authors ... found themselves puzzled by, and sometimes uneasy with, the use of psychological concepts in contemporary neuroscience.... The unease was produced by a suspicion that in some cases concepts were misconstrued, or misapplied, or stretched beyond their defining conditions of application. And the more we probed, the more convinced we became that, despite the impressive advances in cognitive neuroscience, all was not well with the general theorising.[7]

They noted that the great advances in neuroscience made in the beginning of the twentieth century by Charles Sherrington and some of his protégés and colleagues, Edgar Adrian (with whom Sherrington shared the Nobel Prize in 1932), John Eccles and Wilder Penfield, nonetheless left a battery of conceptual questions known as mind-body or mind-brain problems. Many were based on the Cartesian dualism that most of those early twentieth-century scientists held. When that dualism rightly collapsed, no doubt partly from the philosophical considerations outlined in the previous chapter, Bennett and Hacker believed it often led to a new form of dualism, when what had been described as the dualism of mind and body became a new dualism of brain and body.

> Sherrington and his pupils Eccles and Penfield cleaved to a form of dualism in their reflections on the relationship between their neurological discoveries and human perceptual and cognitive capacities. Their successors rejected dualism – quite rightly. But the predicates which dualists ascribe to the

immaterial mind, the third generation of brain neuroscientists applied unreflectively to the brain instead.[8]

Of course, brain and body are both physical objects, which stops that view being dualistic in quite the same way as the Cartesian mind-body dualism, but it is that new dualism that Bennett and Hacker question.

That led to their first concern, the locating in part of an organism what actually belongs to the whole, which they saw as an example of the mereological fallacy. When, for example, some neuroscientists attribute to the brain activities that are essentially activities of the whole human being, Bennett and Hacker certainly recognize that the brain is involved in thinking, but rather than saying as some neuroscientists do "the brain thinks" they believe it is far more accurate to say a human being thinks, using his brain but also all the information he receives from all other parts of the body, not least of all his or her genetic inheritance.

Secondly, what is the nature of memory? They question the language used by LeDoux when he writes that he has learned things and they are *stored in the brain*.[9] They write,

One can store smells in bottles, write down the meaning of words in dictionaries, and codify the rules of games in documents which can be stored – but one cannot *store* smells, meanings of words, or rules *in a* brain! Of course, what LeDoux means is that there are things he can remember – and that is right; where he errs is in the supposition that in order to be able to remember them, he must have stored them in his brain (or anywhere else).[10] The thought that to remember is to store something confuses retention with storage. To remember is to retain. But although storage may sometimes imply retention, retention does not imply storage. Memory, being the retention of knowledge acquired, is the retention of an ability to just the extent that knowledge itself is an ability – but it is not the storage of an ability.[11]

Their primary objection to that notion is that it might be considered as encoding information obtained in some way from the body, and then *storing* the neural record in the brain. This is clearly a very technical discussion, and I am not in a position to make any personal judgment on the matter, but the general reader should at least be aware of the debate.

Thirdly, and most fundamentally, they dispute the reductionism that is expressed by some neuroscientists. Francis Crick once wrote "your joys and sorrows, your memories and your ambitions, your sense of personal identity and free will, are in fact no more than the behavior of a vast assembly of nerve cells and their associated molecules."[12] Colin Blakemore expressed a similar statement. "All our actions are products of our brains.... We *feel* ourselves, usually, to be in control of our actions, but that feeling is itself a product of the brain, whose machinery has been designed, on the basis of its functional utility, by means of natural selection."[13]

Bennett and Hacker describe reductionism as "a single unifying explanation of a type of phenomenon."[14] What Crick and Blakemore say may certainly contain scientific truth, but the problem is when it is considered to be the whole and only truth. No doubt the minds and brains of a Mozart or a Beethoven, or even of Jesus Christ or the Buddha, were subject to such constraints, but to describe them as "no more than that" is to ignore the influence of music or religion on human life more generally. That is the reductionist error. In that connection it is interesting to note that Martin Rees, a former President of the Royal Society, who describes himself as "a practicing but unbelieving Christian" comments that mathematics is the language of science, but music may be the language of religion.[15]

Bennett and Hacker believe that reductionist error is

demonstrated when the American philosopher Wilfred Sellars says "in the dimension of describing and explaining the world, science is the measure of all things, of what is that it is and of what is not that it is not."[16] They comment,

> There is no such thing as explaining the world, only different ways of explaining different phenomena in the world.... Law, economics and sociology no less than physics describes and explains physical phenomena and chemistry describes and explains chemical phenomena. Within their proper domains, the social sciences are no less a measure of what is and what is not. And history, which is neither a natural nor a social science, is a measure of what was that it was and of what was not and that is was not. Moreover, there is no prospect whatsoever that legal, economic, sociological and historical phenomena should be explained by, let alone be reducible to, any natural or biological science. It is grotesque to suggest that these subjects are all pseudo-sciences or mere fables, enmeshed in a vacuous and obsolete vocabulary.[17]

I believe Bennett and Hacker are correct in their concerns, and many of the others that are contained in their book, and the conclusions of neuroscientists need to be examined with care in the light of their philosophical suppositions. But I also note that Bennett and Hacker do not dispute that contemporary neuroscientists are right in rejecting any sort of mind/body dualism. The human mind, which certainly involves the use of the physical brain but also information from the rest of the body, is a mysterious and complex thing, but it is part of that psychosomatic unity that is a human being. When a human body dies then so does the mind and the brain of that person. That does not mean the memory of them in other people ceases, and in that sense their minds and their thoughts are continued in others, which is the subject of a later chapter. But death is death.

Neuroscience and NDEs

Returning to the question of neurological explanations of NDEs one significant exponent is Dr Susan Blackmore, a Visiting Professor of Psychology at the University of Plymouth, who also refers to Out-of-Body Experiences (OBEs). When she was an undergraduate at Oxford, she experienced an OBE while under the influence of drugs. For a long time she believed in some of the more exotic explanations of them such as the existence of astral bodies, but the more research she did the more convinced she became that neurological explanations are most likely.

> NDErs describe clear states of consciousness with lucid reasoning and memory when their brain is severely impaired or even in a state of clinical death... How could a clear consciousness outside one's body be experienced at the moment when the brain no longer functions during a period of clinical death with a flat EEG?... The problem here is that we do not know whether NDEs take place just before the crisis, during it, or just after it, or even during the process of trying to describe it to someone else. If clear consciousness were really possible with a completely flat EEG this would indeed change our view of the mind-brain relationship, but so far this has not been demonstrated.

She describes her own Dying Brain Hypothesis.

> Severe stress, extreme fear and cerebral anoxia all cause cortical disinhibition and uncontrolled brain activity, and we already have most of the ideas needed to understand why this should cause NDEs. Tunnels and lights are frequently caused by disinhibition in visual cortex, and similar noises occur during sleep paralysis. OBEs and life reviews can be induced by temporal lobe stimulation, and the positive emotions and lack of pain have been attributed to the action of endorphins

and encephalins – endogenous opiates which are widely distributed in the limbic system and released under stress. The visions of other worlds and spiritual beings might be real glimpses into another world, but against that hypothesis is evidence that people generally describe other worlds that fit their cultural upbringing. For example, Christians report seeing Jesus, angels, and a door or gate into heaven, while Hindus are more likely to meet the king of the dead and his messengers, the Yamdoots.[18]

A combination of all of those effects may well produce many of the elements of NDEs, which in some ways is like having a particularly vivid dream. Blackmore agrees such experiences can have a very positive effect on people, but while many of the patients think they have encountered a world beyond this one she does not believe in such an explanation; rather she recognizes that the vivid nature of such an experience can lead an individual to review what is important in their lives and may well make them less obsessed by practical matters like money or status and more valuing of friendship and living creatively for the rest of their lives. All of these factors have led her and others to think that NDEs may have a totally neurological explanation, although Parnia notes they do not always fit well with the circumstances surrounding some NDEs. Parnia's own conclusion on brain-based theories is "Although I could see that the brain-based theories discussed in the scientific literature had been developed rationally and eloquently, as they stood they did not seem sufficient to account for the NDE phenomenon. I had no doubt that the brain was involved with the near death experiences, but there had to be other explanations."[19] Blackmore would disagree.

Parnia believes there is a need for further research, and says he wishes to keep an open mind on the different explanations, but he believes this whole matter is an area that may throw light on one of the critical scientific questions of our time, what causes the phenomenon of consciousness and what is the relationship of the mind to the brain.

I think that NDEs hold the key to finally solving this mystery. In studying them further we will be able to discover the true nature of the relationship between the mind and the brain and answer the wider questions regarding the existence of an afterlife. Then we can at least live our lives with the knowledge of what fate will bring to us all.[20]

Keeping an open mind may be admirable, but it is more difficult if the overwhelming majority view of other scientists is different. Believing the mind and the brain (and hence the body) are distinct is often described as dualism, and believing they are one is normally known as monism. While there certainly are some who argue for at least the possibility of the mind being more than the brain and that something like the mind continues through and after death there are far more scientists who are very doubtful about that.

Careful research into the phenomena is advocated, but there are at least two problems. First, research would involve someone who is dying having their brain activity monitored by a scanner during the process of dying and getting any medical ethics committee to agree to that is unlikely. Secondly, people do not die of near-death experiences, so getting funding for any major research project is unlikely, especially as there is a significant body of neuroscientists who believe that any such experiments are unlikely to produce any definite positive result.

In 2014 Parnia found one case that was validated using auditory stimuli during cardiac arrest, but one case at the edge of what science can determine is scarcely enough to show the answer to the whole question of the nature of consciousness. It is inevitable that the personal views of those discussing such matters are reflected in their responses. This does not mean questioning their academic integrity, although one well-known psychologist on the skeptical side of the debate, an American Professor of Psychology James Alcock has described much of the discussion surrounding this as "based on belief in search of data rather than observation in search of explanation." While there are some medically qualified researchers who believe they can prove that life exists after death, I cannot help noticing that the vast majority of neuroscientists think the mind is certainly at the least very heavily dependent on the brain if not even identical to it. We also all experience dreams, which are clearly caused by what is happening in our minds, and they may even be recalled vividly, so NDEs may well be a sort of dream.

The whole issue of the mind/brain relationship continues to be discussed and Susan Blackmore writes about the American philosopher Daniel Dennett's description of what he calls the Cartesian Theatre.

As we have seen there are many dualists among NDE researchers, but in the rest of neuroscience, psychology and philosophy there are very few. Most of these people believe that all experience depends on brain events.... If experience and brain events are inseparable then at the very earliest the awareness of wanting to act would have to start at the same time as the brain events which gave rise to that awareness. More likely some build-up in those events would be required to produce conscious experience.... So if that is obvious why were the arguments so heated and protracted? I think because many scientists, while professing to have rejected dualism, still live in the illusion of Dennett's Cartesian Theatre. It feels as though there is some central place where it all happens; a place where 'I' am; a place to which all the incoming signals come and a place from where 'I' send out the instructions to 'my' body and to the world. But there is no such place. The brain is a complicated system, doing lots of things in parallel, and making lots of decisions at once. There is no one person in there doing it all. Decisions are the consequence of lots and lots of parallel processes coming together to produce an action, a word or a remembered sequence. Am I saying, then, that every time I think I have made a decision, it was actually an illusion? 'I' didn't really make it? Yes – if by 'I' you mean something separate from the rest of the system, then that is precisely what I am saying.[21]

That was written in 1993 and since then investigations of the workings of the brain and the nature of consciousness have continued. In 2005 Susan Blackmore wrote in the OUP series of Very Short Introductions a book entitled *Consciousness* and in 2016 Richard Passingham, Emeritus Professor of Cognitive Neuroscience at Oxford University wrote in the same series *Cognitive Neuroscience*. He outlines one of the developments in neuroscience that have occurred in the last thirty years, functional magnetic brain imaging (fMRI). There are estimated to be about a hundred billion neurons in the human brain, and MRI scanning of the inner workings of the brain by electrodes placed on the scalp can record the activation of parts of the brain by the increased use of oxygen. Since the activities of different parts of the brain are now quite well understood the increased activation shows which function of the brain is being used.

One of the tests that both Passingham and Blackmore describe is the so-called Libet test, devised by a neuroscientist called Benjamin Libet. While someone's brain was subject to an MRI scan they were asked to carry out an action of moving their forefinger and observing a clock with a fast moving light going round the clock. They were asked to note where the light was when they made the decision to move their finger. The surprising result is that the brain scan showed relevant brain activity started some 200 to 300 milliseconds *before* they were aware of making their decision.

The significance of this discovery has been disputed, not least of all by Bennett and Hacker.[22] Some have held that it shows human beings have no free will but simply follow events in the brain, although that was not Libet's own conclusion. The brain might make an initial decision but there is what some have called "free won't," a human being through the brain can then take notice of other factors operating and decide not to do something. In the relatively trivial decisions of the brain in the Libet test of moving a finger that may not be very significant, but what happens when one person through brain activity sees the advantage of doing one action, but then brings to the fore memories that reveal conflict with remembered previous decisions, which may be expressions of firm moral principles? Making a decision in such circumstances may still be an exercise involving myriads of activities by neurons in the brain, but that does not mean the mind and the brain are distinct. Passingham comments "So before a voluntary action there is brain activity of which we are unaware. This certainly posed a problem for those philosophers who take the dualist position as advocated by Descartes. Dualism must hold that awareness occurs either *before* or at the very least *at the same time*. For a dualist an action can be said to be free if *I* will it, not my brain. The problem is that the results of the Libet test appear to show my brain dictating to me. For someone who is not a dualist there is no 'me' apart from my brain and my body; and if so, there is no 'me' for the brain to push about. So long as the brain is healthy, the actions that the brain generates are taken to be the actions that the person generates."[23]

I have reflected on the notion of there being no "me" described by both Passingham and Blackmore in the light of the process of writing this book, for who is the "I" that is writing it? Obviously I have been influenced by much that I have learnt from academic study, and I hope in the process have acquired some things that help me to lay out reasonably coherently the conclusions I come to, although that is for others to judge. But I am also aware that many other things have influenced me, the views of respected teachers, reading, watching films and plays, discussions with friends, and ultimately deciding not just what I think is right, but also what I feel is right. Although in some ways what they say is counter-intuitive, nonetheless it feels to me that Blackmore and Passingham are correct when they imply the "I" who writes this book is not something separate from the rest of the whole system that is me.

As we shall see later some theologians, not just Paul Balham but also Keith Ward and Richard Swinburne nonetheless believe the mind is other than the brain. Ward in particular wonders how something made of matter like the brain can make the major decisions in life that we all need to make. An American theologian David Bentley Hart makes a similar point in *The Experience of God*. He states that it is a principle of the mechanistic vision of reality that material forces are essentially mindless, intrinsically devoid of purpose, and that complex rational organization is not a property naturally residing in material reality. It can only be imposed on material reality. "Consciousness would appear to be everything that, according to the principles of mechanism, matter is not: directed, purposive, essentially rational."[24] He concludes "The difference in kind between the material structure of the brain and the subjective structure of consciousness remains fixed and inviolable, and so the precise relation between them cannot be defined, or even isolated as an object of scientific scrutiny."[25]

A contrary view, which probably represents that of many neuroscientists, is presented by the neurosurgeon Henry Marsh in his book *Do No Harm*.

Everything we think and feel is no more or no less that the electrochemical chatter of our nerve cells. Our sense of self, our feelings and our thoughts, our love for others, our hopes and ambitions, our hopes and fears all die when our brains die. Many people deeply resent this view of things, which not only deprives us of life after death but also seems to downgrade thoughts to mere electrochemistry and reduces us to no more than automats or machines. Such people are profoundly mistaken, since what it really does is upgrade matter into something infinitely mysterious that we do not understand. There are a hundred billion nerve cells in our brains. Does each one have a fragment of consciousness within it? How many nerve cells do we require to be conscious or to feel pain? Or does consciousness and thought reside in the electrochemical impulses that join those billion of cells together? Is a snail aware? Does it feel pain when you crush it underfoot? Nobody knows.[26]

Marsh's first sentence no doubt reflects the reductionism that Bennett and Hacker rightly object to, but that does not undermine the rest of the quotation. My own personal conclusion is therefore that the arguments for holding that the mind and the brain are at the very least in close connection are far stronger than those who wish to assert that they are independent. It is, for example, quite possible to describe the brain as the physical object that is in our heads, and the mind includes all the information that is provided by other parts of our bodies which is then processed in some way by the brain. Knowledge of how the brain works and is integrated with the rest of our bodies is being investigated all the time. The physiology of memory, for example, is now well understood, with even an identification being made between different sorts of memories and different parts of the brain although Bennett and Hacker dispute some of the details about the storage of memory. However, it is also now understood that when brain death finally occurs the brain reasonably quickly collapses and a person's memory is no more. Since memory is such a fundamental part of what we are, the loss of it makes it difficult to see how anything that we might consider to be the essential us continues.

This points to a very major issue facing those who advocate traditional Christian belief, possibly on a par with earlier apparent conflicts between science and religion. The two most obvious examples of such past conflicts are the Copernican revolution, when the original suggestion that the earth revolved round the sun rather than vice versa was considered by many including the Catholic Church to be a heresy and then the Darwinian revolution when it was suggested that evolution was the mechanism which brought about human life.

In the case of Copernicus, his theory was published in 1543 but only gained greater awareness when Galileo advocated heliocentrism over 50 years later. This led to the Inquisition deciding it was false in 1616 and summoning Galileo to Rome in 1633, declaring him guilty of suspected heresy. It took a further nearly 200 years before the prohibition by the Catholic Church on publishing Copernicus' work was repealed and the Catholic Church officially changed its mind.

Darwin's *On the Origin of Species* was published in 1859 and some Christians, most notably Frederick Temple, then Bishop of Exeter and later Archbishop of Canterbury, accepted "the doctrine of Evolution is in no sense antagonistic to the teachings of Religion."[27] Others were far more condemnatory from the start and some still are today. The Roman Catholic Church was more circumspect, maybe learning from its mistakes over Copernicus. It made no formal declaration on the subject until 1950, and even then it was only a very cautious acceptance of it. The history of the Church's engagement with major scientific developments is, to say the least, patchy.

It will therefore be interesting to observe how far today the church is able to engage seriously with some of the proposals coming from neuroscience, particularly the notion that dualism in the Cartesian sense is wrong and that the physical brain is the key to understanding the nature of human beings and consciousness. If that is the case it certainly undermines much that has traditionally been said about the soul and the mind.

Conclusion

On the central matter of this chapter I conclude that while the memory of us in other people's minds may well continue for some time, and to that extent we may continue to live in their memories, any continuation of personal consciousness seems to me to be very unlikely. When the brain dies all that it contains dies with it. It is for that reason I conclude that despite the reality of NDEs, their possible beneficial effect and the continued debate, death is death.

In the next chapter we shall observe that some notable Christians have already engaged with such issues with the seriousness they deserved. They raise some major questions about what can realistically be believed about what happens to us when we die.

Chapter 5 Endnotes

1   Parnia S. *What happens When We Die*. Hay Books; 2005. p. 15–16.

2   p. 19.

3   Fenwick P, Fenwick E. *The Truth in the Light. An investigation of over 300 near-death experiences*. Headline Book Publishing; 1995.

4   *Making Sense of Death and Immortality*. SPCK Modern Church Series; 2013.

5   Sartori P. *The Near-Death Experiences of Hospitalized Intensive Care Patients: A five-year clinical study*. Lampeter: Edwin Mellen Press; 2008.

6   Parnia. p. 34.

7   Bennett MR, Hacker PMS. *Philosophical Foundations of Neuroscience*. Blackwell; 2003. p. 1.

8   Ibid p. 72.

9   LeDoux J. *Emotional Brain*. Weidenfeld & Nicholson; 1998. p. 179.

10 ibid p.159.

11 ibid p. 164.

12 Crick F. *The Astonishing Hypothesis*. London: Touchstone; 1995. p. 3.

13 Blakemore C. *The Mind Machine*. London: BBC Publications; 1988.

14 ibid p. 357.

15 Rees M. *On the Future: Prospects for Humanity*. Princeton University Press; 2018. p. 199 and 168.

16 Sellars W. *Science, Perception and Reality; Empiricism and the philosophy of mind*. London: Routledge and Kegan Paul; 1963. p. 173.

17 ibid p. 373f.

18 Blackmore S. *Consciousness: An Introduction*. Second Edition. Hodder; 2010. p. 412 f.

19 Parnia. p. 32.

20 p. 200.

21 Blackmore S. *Dying to Live.* Harper Collins; 1993. p. 237.

22 Bennett M. *Philosophical Foundations of Neuroscience* pp. 228–231.

23 Passingham R. *Cognitive Neuroscience.* OUP; p. 85 f. The whole experiment is explained pp. 83–87. Susan Blackmore explains the same experiment and some of the criticisms of it in *Consciousness.* OUP; pp. 87–91. Both conclude that dualism is incorrect.

24 Bentley Hart D. *The Experience of God.* London: Yale University Press; 2013. p. 154.

25 p. 157.

26 Marsh H. *Do No Harm.* Phoenix edition. 2014. p. 200.

27 Temple F. *The Relations between Religion and Science: Eight Lectures Preached Before the University of Oxford in the Year 1884.* London: Macmillan; p. 107.

Chapter 6

Christianity since 1900

Since the beginning of the twentieth century debate about life after death within the Christian Church has been more varied than possibly many realize, although some simply advocated what they saw as the traditional view.

Certainly in the first half of the century there were those who believed the basic Cartesian dualism that held sway until the 1950s. W. R. Matthews (1881–1973) was a Professor of Theology at King's College, London before becoming Dean of St Paul's Cathedral in 1934, where he remained in post for thirty-three years. In 1936 he wrote *The Hope of Immortality* and argued that hope for an existence beyond death was widespread and, although there was clearly interplay between mind and body, Plato was essentially right in thinking that mind is a higher kind of existence than matter and body. He also believed there were intimations of immortality in psychic phenomena, although he did not believe they were conclusive. What was perhaps more surprising was that when he revised his book in 1966 with an additional chapter responding to some of the questions he had been asked, he made no reference to the attack on Cartesian dualism advanced by Ryle and Wittgenstein in the 1950s.

Matthews based his belief in the natural immortality of human beings on his belief in God and resurrection. "In every rational being there is the seed of immortality. There is an element, which is not subject to the change and decay of time.... What we can say of every rational being is that he is potentially immortal in the full sense of the word: his nature is such that he is capable of receiving the gift of eternal life."[1] Matthews was quite prepared to see notions of Hell as only symbolic of an eternal separation from God based on the choice of the individual human being, but he believed that would lead to extinction rather than perpetual punishment. His predecessor at St Paul's, Dean Inge, described Matthews as an "Orthodox Modernist."

Since then there has certainly been widespread discussion within the Christian Church about eschatology. John Macquarrie, a former Lady Margaret Professor of Divinity at Oxford, summarized the overall challenge. "Attempts by theologians even down to modern times to sort out all the elements in the conventional understanding of the Christian hope remind one of the endless modifications and refinements that were made to the Ptolemaic system of astronomy until finally it was abandoned for the vastly simpler Copernican scheme. Something like a Copernican revolution seems to be demanded of Christian eschatology."[2] David Edwards, a former Provost of Southwark Cathedral, in his own book on beliefs about death and its consequences, endorsed that view.[3]

Within the Christian Church since the middle of the twentieth century there have been and still are serious debates on five interrelated issues.

1. *The first fundamental one is how do we understand what a human being is. Should Cartesian dualism be replaced by the notion that human beings are a psychosomatic unity, with mind and body so intimately related that it is impossible realistically to think of them being separate?* There are differing views.

Some Christian theologians certainly retain a form of the dualism that Ryle and Wittgenstein challenged. Richard Swinburne, Emeritus Professor of the Philosophy of the Christian Religion at Oxford, recently argued that each human being had a soul whose character was shown through the decisions that person made and the beliefs they held.[4] He acknowledges that the majority of philosophers today do not accept Cartesian dualism, but he prefers to believe in what he describes as "substance dualism." "Each of us living on earth consists of two substances (two distinct parts) – body and soul, but the part that makes us who we are is our soul. Bodies keep us alive, and by enabling us to interact with each other and the world make our lives greatly worth living; but souls are what we essentially are. By some miracle we might continue to exist without our body, but no miracle would make it possible for us to exist without our soul – because for each of us our soul is the one essential part of us."[5] He recognizes that the word "soul" may have religious overtones that some would object to, so suggests an alternative might be "self." In the rest of his book he works out that theory with remarkable thoroughness, including a detailed examination of the relationship of what he describes as "brain events" and "mental events," and his purpose is to show that "substance dualism" is the best scientific explanation of what human beings are.

Some other theologians agree. Keith Ward, a former Regius Professor of Divinity at Oxford, takes a similar line. "It may seem that my own account of minds or souls as continuing and partly self-directing streams of experience verges on this sort of Cartesian dualism."[6] In Chapter 5 I quoted the American theologian, Bentley Hart, who certainly holds to a dualism between the material and the mental and as we saw in Chapter 4, Anthony Kenny recognized that it remains an influential concept even though personally he does not accept it.

But that approach was certainly not universal among Christian theologians. John Macquarrie wrote "A self or soul seems to be of a quite different order from a physical body, and when we attempt to grasp it as an object of investigation, it eludes us, for it is just not objectifiable in the ways bodies are. But to try to solve the problem by moving in the direction of a Cartesian dualism seems to me to be mistaken.... Objections to a dualism of soul and body have multiplied in modern philosophy, and I think that cumulatively they make the doctrine highly improbable."[7]

Karl Rahner (1904–1984), whom many would maintain was

the leading Roman Catholic theologian of the twentieth century, wrote:

> We have to consider here what the basic knowledge is which Christian anthropology has about man. If we maintain, for example, that man ... really is a corporeal person with an absolute and ultimately irreversible unity of matter and spirit ... this must necessarily say something about the salvation of the single and total person. Christian anthropology would be incomplete and even false if it wanted to understand the individual's final state merely as the salvation of an abstract human soul.[8]

He goes on to say that man is an absolute unity which cannot simply be split up into body and soul and that must apply to any eschatological statements about the fulfillment of the soul or the body. "It is ultimately superfluous to ask what a person does while his body is in the grave and his soul is already with God ... this duality cannot be understood as indiscriminate statements about quite different realities."[9]

Personally, I find the arguments of Macquarrie and Rahner far more persuasive than the assertions of Swinburne and Ward. I do not believe we can realistically talk about "the soul"; the bodily nature of human beings and the fact that body and mind are intimately bound together we cannot ignore. However, I also note the criticisms of some aspects of modern neuroscience advanced by Bennett and Hacker in Chapter 5 show they are certainly anxious to maintain that decisions are taken by the full human being and not just by the brain. This might go some way towards meeting the issues Swinburne raises, but that did not stop Bennett and Hacker disputing dualism. Seeing human beings as psychosomatic unities is certainly the majority view among philosophers and neuroscientists today and I believe they are right.

2. *What is meant by eternity?*

In the 1920s Wittgenstein made the following observation: "Death is not an event in life: we do not live to experience death. If we take eternity to mean not infinite temporal duration but timelessness, then eternal life belongs to those who live in the present. Our life has no end in just the way in which our visual field has no limits."[10] Some theologians also took up that notion in the twentieth century.

Karl Barth was probably the most influential Protestant theologian of the twentieth century and was an exponent of what became known as Dialectical Theology or the "theology of crisis." Emerging from the horrors of the First World War his *Epistle to the Romans* (1918) challenged the pre-war liberal view of eschatology as the gradual realization in history of the Kingdom of God. Rather, Barth held that the "wholly other" God broke into time and history where every moment could become the eschatological moment when eternity broke in with judgment and grace. Rudolph Bultmann, who expressed his radicalism through his program of "demythologization," also shared that view. He believed the whole language of eschatology needed to be translated into a mythology that made sense for contemporary man, which inevitably included for him a new way of looking at death. He summarized his view at the end of the 1955 Gifford Lectures:

> *The meaning in history lies always in the present,* and when the present is conceived as the eschatological present by Christian faith the meaning in history is realized. Man who complains; 'I cannot see meaning in history, and therefore my life, interwoven in history, is meaningless', is to be admonished: do not look around yourself into universal history; you must look into your own personal history. Always in your present lies the meaning in history, and you cannot see it as a spectator, but only in your responsible decisions. In every

moment slumbers the possibility of being the eschatological moment. You must awaken it.[11]

In other words, eschatology is about now, not the future. Karl Barth was even more adamant. He said that believing in an afterlife is "pursing pagan dreams of good times after death."[12] He maintained the New Testament teaches that time comes to an end on the last day at the "final trump," when "time shall be no more." For Barth, there was no question of the continuation into an indefinite future of a somewhat altered life. The New Testament hope for the other side of death is very different from that. What it looks forward to is the "eternalizing" of this ending life. He wrote:

Eternal life is not another and second life, beyond the present one. It is this life, but the reverse side which God sees although it is yet hidden from us – this life in relation to what he has done for the whole world, and therefore for us too, in Jesus Christ. We thus wait and hope, even in view of our own death, for our manifestation with Him, with Jesus Christ who was raised from the dead, in the glory of not only the judgment but also the grace of God.[13]

Rahner also broadly followed Wittgenstein's notion when he considered the implications of any conception of life beyond death. He wrote about Death and Eternity.

If we have to speak in Christian eschatology of the dead who are still alive, we have to say first of all what this means, or, better, what it does not mean. It does not mean that things continue on after death as though, as Feuerbach put it, we only change horses and then ride on ... No, in this respect death marks the end of the whole person. If we simply have time continue beyond a person's death, and have the 'soul' survive in this time, so that new time comes to be instead of time being subsumed into its final and definitive reality, then we get into insuperable difficulties today both in understanding what the Christian doctrine really means and also in living it existentially..... In reality eternity comes to be in time as time's mature fruit, an eternity which does not really continue on beyond experienced time. Rather eternity subsumes time by being liberated from time ... Eternity is not an infinitely long mode of pure time, but rather it is a mode of the spiritual freedom, which has been exercised in time, and therefore it can be understood only from a correct understanding of human freedom. A time, which does not exist as the seedbed of spirit and freedom, does not offer us any eternity.[14]

As we shall see Hebblethwaite and others disputed the notion that eternity was not temporal, but that will be considered after this examination of the five main areas of debate.

3. *What is the primary focus of eschatology?*

John Robinson's *In the End God* was published in 1968, five years after *Honest to God* had established him in the public mind as a radical theologian. He stressed that salvation could never simply be for the individual but for the whole world and his basic concern was to talk about God rather than individual life after death.

The doctrine of the resurrection of the body is the doctrine of the redemption and replacement of one solidarity by another – the body of the old mortality by the body of Christ. It is an assertion that no individual can be saved apart from the whole. Through his body he is organically linked with all other life and all other matter in the universe. There is no redemption for the individual *out* of this mass, but only in and with it. The Christian gospel is not of rescuing individuals out of nature and history ... but the redeeming of the myriad of relationships of creation into a new heaven and a new earth, the city of God, the body of Christ.... The doctrine of the resurrection of the body is misunderstood if it is regarded as a preview of what the future holds in store for the individual. Information about this no more forms part of the Christian revelation than prognostications about the end of history. Of course, *something* must actually happen to the individual, just as the world must end in one-way and not another. But it is not the function of Christian theology in either case to assert what this will be. The locus of its interest lies not in the future, but in the present. The doctrine of bodily resurrection is not forecast but myth. That is to say, it is the representation, in this as the most scientific form, of a truth, which is internal to the Biblical understanding of God's relationship to man, the truth, namely, that the *whole* of God's workmanship is of eternal value to himself and cannot ultimately be lost.[15]

The year before *In the End God* was published Robinson wrote *But That I Can't Believe,* most of which originally appeared in the Sunday Mirror written for a popular audience. He describes what he thought was many young people's reaction to death. "Death may be the end. So what? And as for the Christian faith, it must either show itself to be true in this life, or not at all."[16] As he expanded later, the New Testament doesn't rest its hope on anything *going on* from this life to another.

Nor does it say there's a spark of immortality in us that never dies. In fact, if one thing is certain, it is that we die. And that is the end of everything that depends on continuities from this body. Belief in the resurrection of flesh and blood, and consequent religious prejudice against cremation is superstition. The Christian symbol of resurrection (rather than survival or immortality) means that death marks a real break. What lies on the other side of it I literally cannot imagine. And I am not going to get distracted by worrying about it. All I know is that God lies the other side of it – as he lies this side of it ... death cannot have the last word.... For the rest, with so many of my generation, I am prepared to be agnostic. I just cannot imagine an after-life, and it doesn't much help if I try.... The Bible, like all ancient literature, projects pictures (not, of course, to be taken literally) of 'another world', to which people go when they die. The pictures are simply ways of trying to make the spiritual truth real and vivid to the imagination. If they help, well and good. But a lot of people today find it difficult to *visualize* anything after death. I am among them. But our commitment to Christ is not for that reason in doubt. Our concern is with working out that commitment here and now, with what eternal life – real life – means in this situation. Of course we can set no bounds to it. As St Paul says, 'If in this life only we have hoped in Christ, we are of all men most foolish'. But nothing turns on what happens after death. For whatever happens, we already know a reality we cannot escape and from which nothing can separate.[17]

John Macquarrie made a related observation:

It ought to be said that any worthy conception of the ultimate destiny of the individual must be purged from every trace of egocentricity. Often one has the impression that arguments for immortality or for the continued existence of the individual are infected by a wrong kind of self-regard. If the fulfillment of individual existence is to be somehow like God, then this means learning the love that looses itself by pouring itself out; and this might mean that the individual existent must be prepared to vanish utterly into the whole, and for the sake of the whole.[18]

Later in that chapter, which was concerned with The Last Things, he wrote of how the kingdom of God could be conceived. "It would be a commonwealth of free beings, united in Being and with each other through love, yet since this is the love that lets-be, preserving a diversity that heightens the value of unity far above any undifferentiated unity."[19] But in his later book, as noted also in the following section, he wrote "the past that has perished for us is still present in God.... Could we suppose then that our destiny as individuals is not to live on as immortal souls or to be provided with new bodies, but to be summed up or gathered up in the experience of God as the people we are or have been in our several segments of time and in our bodies?"[20]

Dr Norman Pittenger, an Anglican priest and former Chairman of the Theological Commission of the World Council of Churches, who in retirement lived as a senior member of King's College, Cambridge, pursued a similar theme on the centrality of God in *After Death Life in God*. He was more definite than Robinson in rejecting any notion of an afterlife for the individual. "Not only do we *all* die, which is obvious enough, but *all of us* also dies, which to many may not appear obvious. We die, body and mind, even 'soul' (if that word is right to use here); and all talk in the world about 'immortality of the soul' will not deliver us from this kind of finality."[21]

He approached theology from the perspective of Process Theology from A. N. Whitehead's philosophy, and what is distinctive is his notion of the memory of God. "God remembers: and what is in the divine memory is no incidental or accidental matter, but the very reality of creation kept in him for ever and hence 'come alive', as we might put it, in God's on-going reality."[22] He quotes with approval David Edwards, writing when he was Dean of Norwich. "Certainly one great advantage of thinking about God's memory of us is that it helps us to see that our eternal life is more than this life going on for ever and ever: it is a share in God's life and God's glory, when nothing is between God and us."[23]

Pittenger continued:

> In this sense, then, Jesus Christ himself is remembered by
> God; and those who are 'in Christ' ... are also remembered....
> I am concerned that it is this which is the absolutely central
> Christian affirmation, not least of all because the stress is
> laid on God and God's action, rather than on ourselves and
> our 'conscious' awareness of being remembered. Certainly it
> is legitimate to entertain the pious hope than in our being
> thus remembered there may be some kind of 'conscious'
> awareness. But it is not legitimate, and to my mind quite
> mistaken, to talk as if without such an awareness on our part
> there is only a 'second best'. To be incorporated into the life of
> Christ and hence to be taken into the divine remembrance of
> Christ here is the heart of genuinely Christian hope, whatever
> else we may think proper to desire and (in a secondary sense)
> to hope for.[24]

*4. A further fundamental issue in the twentieth century and since is
what can we realistically believe about God?*

The notion of God was debated in much of the last century
and is still now. There were great differences between equally
distinguished theologians. Maurice Wiles' view of the action
of God in the world[25] was certainly challenged by his successor
as Regius Professor of Divinity at Oxford, Keith Ward. What
someone believes about God may make a difference to what they
believe about life after death.

The matter may be best examined by considering the
differences between John Macquarrie and Keith Ward, who
retired as Regius Professor of Divinity at Oxford in 2004. He
wrote widely on the subject of God over his academic career and
in 2017 produced *The Christian Idea of God*. He acknowledges that
his notion of God is but one way of thinking about God within

the Christian tradition, and in his appreciation of Macquarrie,[26] published after Macquarrie's death in 2007, he noted their different conclusions. They start from different philosophical positions. Macquarrie wrote from an existentialist background. The founder of existentialism is often considered to be Søren Kierkegaard although he never used the word himself. He proposed that each individual is solely responsible for giving meaning to life and living it passionately and sincerely, or "authentically." Kierkegaard wrote "If I wish to preserve myself in faith I must constantly be intent upon holding fast the objective uncertainty, so as to remain out upon the deep, over seventy thousand fathoms of water, still preserving my faith." Existentialism says philosophical thinking begins with the human subject—not merely the thinking subject, but the acting, feeling, living human individual. While the predominant value of existentialist thought is commonly acknowledged to be freedom, its primary virtue is authenticity. Many existentialists have regarded traditional systematic or academic philosophies as too abstract and remote from concrete human experience.

Ward, by contrast, starts from what he describes as personal idealism, although he recognizes that "there are not many idealists in modern analytical philosophy, although there are some."[27] As with all idealists he holds that our minds are greater than our brains, which he just sees as a collection of physical parts, and he says we make decisions through our minds. While that involves our brains it also involves something that he chooses to call "a soul." He also believes that God is the Supreme Mind that lies behind the universe, that such a God is a disembodied Mind, that God and the material universe form a unity, though one in which the mental and spiritual aspects have ontological and causal priority. Personally, I am more than happy to say that is "A" Christian Idea of God, but I am far less sure that it can be described as "The" Christian view of God, not least of all because it contrasts so strongly with Macquarrie's view.

Macquarrie held that "Faith is not primarily assent to propositions, but an existential attitude of acceptance and commitment; and that revelation is not primarily given in the form of statements, but it is rather the self-giving or self-communication of being."[28] He followed Aquinas in not believing that God could be understood as *a* being among other beings in the universe, but as Being itself. "As we are all beings we participate in Being itself, and that allows the possibility of a sense of wonder at being at all and an awareness of a graciousness at the heart of being that allows us to be." He notes, however, that is not universal. "Some people have what has all the formal characteristics of a revelation of being, but experience being not as gracious but as alien and without any such content as the religious man ascribes to it."[29]

He describes a progression in the human understanding of God.

The idea of God has undergone many changes in the course of its history. At the *mythological* level, God was perceived anthropomorphically as a being much like ourselves, only more powerful, and he 'dwelt' in a definite place, the top of a mountain, perhaps, or in the sky. At the level of *traditional theism*, the earlier image had been considerably purged. Anthropomorphic elements were toned down in the interests of transcendence, though God was still thought of as a person, but a strange metaphysical person without a body. He was no longer located in the sky, but he 'dwelt' metaphorically beyond the world, though he kept it running and intervened in its affairs when necessary. He was another being in addition to the beings we know in this world. But science has shown us that the world can get along as a self-regulating entity and we do not need to posit some other being beyond it. In any case, such a being would not be an ultimate, because we could still ask about *his* being. Contemporary theology is beginning to move out of the phase in which 'God' meant an exalted being beyond the world. The next phase would seem to be the identification of God with what I have called 'holy being', and we may think of this as the phase of *existential-ontological theism*. So far is it from volatizing or eliminating the idea of God that it makes it possible for this idea to have an ultimacy that it did not have in traditional theism.[30]

He also believed that atheism must be understood in relation to what it denies. He notes that in terms of the view of God in what he called the *mythological* level most people today would be atheists. The denial that God is *a* being would also seem to be atheism to someone who believed in such a view of God. What he has described as *existential-ontological theism* has its own corresponding atheism, which is the denial of the holiness of being, and subsequently the denial that man should have faith in being or take up the attitude of acceptance and commitment before being. He asks "Does therefore God 'exist'? While to say 'God exists' is strictly inaccurate and may be misleading if it makes us think of him as *some* being or other, yet it is more appropriate to say 'God exists' than 'God does not exist', since God's letting be is prior to and the condition of existence of any particular being."[31] He goes on to ask whether this might be considered a variety of "panentheism," which traditionally understood means that God is in everything. He answers his own question "panentheism is really a variety of theism, one which takes care to stress God's immanence equally with his transcendence."[32]

There are certain aspects of each of these views that are common; both, for example, recognize that God can be affected by what happens in the world as God is in a deep relationship with it. But they are also different. Ward's position is possibly more sophisticated than the traditional theism that Macquarrie outlines, but it is obviously closer to that than Macquarrie's existential-ontological theism. But the greatest differences lie in the question of matter and its relationship to the soul. Ward notes that the philosopher John Searle holds that minds cannot exist without matter, and that consciousness is therefore dependent on the human brain. Ward does not agree, but holds what he describes as a less extreme view, that the mental aspect also has a causal role and that each aspect could exist without the other. "It does seem inconceivable that material bodies, with only properties such as mass, spin, charge, position, and momentum, could actually by their own powers bring mental properties into existence."[33] Ward describes the agent of those mental properties as "the soul." Macquarrie does not specifically write about the relationship of mind to brain and does not discuss Searle, who wrote some years after his own two books, but panentheism certainly considers God is in matter. On the subject of "the soul" Macquarrie writes "The conception of a disembodied soul or self is very difficult, since it is precisely through being embodied that we are in a world and with other selves ... there can be no selfhood apart from a world and other selves."[34] In his book *Christian Hope*, Macquarrie says "Human life seems to us to be so bound up with the body that we cannot envisage for it any reality when the body is dissolved."[35] On that basis he finds a reliance on either the immortality of the soul or any sort of physical resurrection impossible to sustain, but as I said in the previous section, he does suggest a third way, which does not deny the finality of death but which recognizes that our perception of the past can change. "What cannot be changed about the past is its factuality ... what has been and what has been done remain. However, though one cannot change the facts of the past, the value of these facts can be changed and often is changed. It is in this sense that one can quite properly say that the past can be healed and transformed."[36]

This contrast becomes even clearer when Ward, in the third

section of his book entitled Supreme Good, considers "the World to Come." He asks "can consciousness and mind exist without a body or, more relevantly, without a brain? It is harder to find instances when it does so, but I think it is easy to think of it doing so.... When humans die, they may continue to have memories and a sense of their own identity."[37] That was obviously different from Macquarrie's view. There remain very conflicting views about the nature of God even, or perhaps especially, among serious Christian theologians.

5. *The relation of theology to other disciplines. How should the Christian Church respond to the insights of other disciplines, whether philosophy, history or science?*

I find Macquarrie's summary compelling. He says that Christian Faith must be coherent with other truths derived from the sciences, from history and other disciplines and continues:

> We cannot, for instance, formulate theological doctrines of creation or providence that are at variance with what we believe about the physical world on scientific grounds. We cannot accept certain reports about the past if these conflict with well-tried findings of historical research. In such areas, it is clear that the criteria for establishing theological truth cannot be different from the criteria used in secular disciplines, and this is important in showing that in each case we are still concerned with *truth*.... In a study where truth is, we hope, always being more fully appropriated but never totally grasped, finality and fixity are signs of error. There must be room for development, for the process of advancing into truth.[38]

That probably most clearly identifies a fundamental difference between two approaches to the question of God. Is God to be found in this world, by a careful analysis of what we observe, but also of what we think and feel? Or is at least some of the content of belief in God to be transferred to another world, the very structure of which might be very different to the world and universe we know? If the latter then of course it can never be disproved. If the structure of such a universe is not only not known to us but is incapable of being known in this life then we have no choice but to accept ultimate ignorance.

However, it is interesting to note the comments of David Edwards, by then Provost of Southwark Cathedral, on two examples of statements about what might be in a world beyond the one we know now. John Polkinghorne, a former President of Queens College, Cambridge and a notable physicist wrote in his *Belief in God in an Age of Science* (1998) "The 'matter' of the world to come, which will be the carrier of this re-embodiment, will be the transformed matter of the present world, itself redeemed by God beyond its cosmic death."[39] Edwards commented "it can be questioned whether any kind of scientific knowledge is relevant to the belief this distinguished scientist holds, for the 'matter' which scientists investigate is, he says, to be 'redeemed' by being 'transformed' and the question remains whether, in that case, it should rightly be called matter."[40]

Then on an earlier expression of Ward's (1998) view about the world to come in his *God, Faith and the New Millennium*, David Edwards believed that Ward earlier in the book had "provided a persuasive restatement of Christian beliefs which takes full account of the findings of natural science about the evolution of the universe and of humankind on this planet. But when he turns to the future he, too, has allowed himself to be in danger of leaving the impression that Christian faith in life after death involves the kind of fantasy that entertains us in science fiction. That cannot be his intention."[41] Interestingly the final chapter in Edward's own book is entitled "Heaven without another world."

Where and how we can find reliable truth about God is the most fundamental theological question of all. In my view carefully investigating the world and universe we know as Macquarrie suggests must be a more reliable guide than speculation about a possible future world, the details of which we cannot know and which may be merely wishful thinking.

Alternative views

That was not the only view of all recent Christian writers on the subject and any examination of twentieth-century theological thought must acknowledge the presence of other points of view. One of the many possibilities I have already considered is Tom Wright's in Chapter 3, but here I examine four others: John Hick's, Brian Hebblethwaite's, Anthony Thistleton's and Dale Allison's, considered in the chronological order in which they were written.

John Hick

John Hick became H. G. Wood Professor of Theology at Birmingham University in 1967 and given the presence of other religious faiths in that city made a significant contribution to inter-faith thought while there. In 1976 his influential book *Death and Eternal Life* [42] was published, at the time one of the most substantial treatments of the subject for some years.

He envisaged the creation by God of a replica person in some other space than the world we know where the person would retain the memories and character traits shown in his life on earth. David Edwards summarized it "He suggested that the old belief about souls being added to new bodies in this world was a mythological expression of the truth that souls are given new bodies in another world. He wrote about the possibility of 'the divine creation in another space of an exact psycho-physical "replica" of the deceased person'". "Resurrected persons", he added later, "would presumably be able to identify each other in the same kind of ways and with a like degree of reassurance as we do now." Edwards commented "But these suggestions seem no less mythological than the beliefs of the past and many questions have been asked about his suggestions. Can we talk meaningfully about 'another space' of which we have no knowledge? What does 'psycho-physical' mean if the new body is neither spiritual nor physical in a sense we can understand? And can a person's identity be preserved by the creation after death of what is only a replica?"

Edwards noted "It may seem that Hick anticipated the force of these questions, for in his book he said plainly that he did not believe that the resurrection of the body would be the final state.... There will be 'a series of lives, each bounded by something analogous to birth and death, lived in other worlds.' The final, heavenly state will lie 'beyond separate ego-existence', when 'it may be that embodiment is no longer necessary.'"[43] That was no doubt developed in response to Hick's knowledge of Eastern visions of re-incarnation, but I am not sure that makes it any more believable.

I had a personal link to John Hick in that he supervised me in philosophy when I was an undergraduate and he was a stimulating supervisor. At the time he was developing his thought in response to the Logical Positivists' view that a statement was only meaningful if it could be verified, and he believed that theological statements could only be verified by what finally happened at the end of all time, or as he called it "eschatological verification." I must confess that stimulating though I found him, I was not convinced by that then and am still not now.

Brian Hebblethwaite

I have quoted extensively from Brian Hebblethwaite's book on Christian Hope, which is a very helpful guide to Christian discussions over many centuries.[44] His final chapter is entitled "A Christian Eschatology for the Twenty-First Century" and I examine it here because I fundamentally disagree with him.

He believes that theodicy, justifying the ways of God in face of the facts of evil, is a central issue. "It is not just the fact that the Christian mind cannot entertain the idea of personal relations between human beings and the God of love being extinguished for ever by death; it is the fact that so many human beings have led stunted, thwarted, and prematurely curtailed lives in the midst of largely unrealized potentialities.... We find ourselves asking why the world is as it is in the first place."[45] He recognized that the early church had very little hope for social transformation of the world and so saw Christian Hope purely in terms of the millennial rule of Christ after the Parousia. But after the conversion of Constantine various forms of a "this-worldly hope" began to emerge although a sober realism about the wickedness of men and women prevailed. That changed in the eighteenth and nineteenth centuries, and although belief in the immortality of the soul remained a common presupposition, most people's hopes – including those of broad sections of the churches – shifted and came to rest on hope for the education of the human race and the gradual realization of an ethical Kingdom of God on earth. He believes it was only in the modern world that a balance had been found between a this-worldly hope and an otherworldly hope. But he also believed that hope for this world requires the ultimate Christian hope if it is to maintain confidence, as well as realism and patience, in the face of otherwise overwhelming odds.

However, as we have seen through the discussions about Barth, Rahner, Macquarrie, Edwards and others, the issue is what the ultimate Christian Hope requires? Can the need for the ultimate only be answered by a temporal hope *after death* or by something *beyond* time, as Wittgenstein understood eternity?

Hebblethwaite certainly recognizes that in this life bounded by birth and death there are the opportunities to forge personal values.

The material creation is a necessary stage, therefore, in the whole creative purpose.... [A]ll the values of human life, at least in the first productive phase of the creative process, are rooted in these conditions of mortality and related to the boundedness of human life.... A serious anthropology ... must reckon with this boundedness of human life. Moreover ... the fact that our lives on earth are lived within the horizon of inevitable death is not a purely negative fact. It gives much of the color, poignancy, and character to the actual values we enjoy as human beings. Secular anthropologists will be liable to assert that all human values are essentially limited and temporary just because of the universal fact of death.... Much recent Christian eschatology (one thinks of Tillich, Rahner, Hartshorne, Jüngel, and Macquarrie) has tended to share this sense of the essential boundedness of the self, and it is one of the reasons why they have questioned the idea of life *after* death. But Christian theology has no business to be following secular anthropology here ... some of the values that ... come to characterize a human life themselves suggest intimations of immortality ... but the main reason ... is in its primary conviction of the reality and nature of God.[46]

Hebblethwaite's main arguments for a temporal hope for the future therefore lie in two convictions, his conception of the nature of God and his perception of the need for a realistic theodicy. Each must be examined.

In section 4 above I outlined what seems the fundamental differences between Macquarrie's and Ward's view of God; Hebblethwaite is obviously more on Ward's side of that debate. My difficulty is that I can see no evidence for why Ward's or Hebblethwaite's view is more true. It requires believing in a God who is going to make some huge transformation of all that we know into some form of "redeemed matter" which cannot be explained, which is in turn capable of maintaining some sort of inexplicable non-physical life in some temporal but endless life. I see no evidence for believing that, so it seems to me to be a view of God for which there is no justification other than a philosophical argument based on nothing substantial.

But Macquarrie and many other serious theologians of the twentieth century including Anglicans such as John Robinson, Maurice Wiles, Geoffrey Lampe and David Jenkins, all of whom held major posts in academic theology, and Roman Catholics such as Hans Küng and Karl Rahner, together provide alternative views of God that seem to me certainly credible, which do not require my believing "half a dozen impossible things before breakfast," and which take the findings of secular disciplines including science with the utmost seriousness. It also takes the thoughts of secular anthropologists seriously because they too are concerned with *truth*. I have no doubt there are some in the church who wish to impose their particular view of God and will happily exclude those who do not share their view, but I believe in an inclusive church that is capable of holding a wide range of opinions even on such a fundamental question as the nature of God.

Hebblethwaite's second argument relates to theodicy. In Chapter One of this book the section on Judaism shows the death of many young Jewish men in the Maccabean Revolt of the second century BCE against the Seleucid Empire produced the argument for belief in life after death at a fairly late stage of the Old Testament. However, as Rabbi Mark Solomon suggested in that same section the Holocaust, with the perceived failure of God to intervene and protect his people, made belief in an afterlife for many Jews a sort of disgraceful cop-out. An American Rabbi Irving Greenberg commented on the decision taken by the Nazi authorities at Auschwitz not to put young Jewish children into the gas chambers, but to throw them alive into the crematoria, and their screams were heard throughout the camp. He wrote "No statement, theological or otherwise, should be made that could not be made with credibility in the presence of the burning children."[47] Could anybody in such circumstances say life after death would provide an adequate response; it is almost blasphemous. Personally, I find the very notion that life after death can produce an adequate theodicy in the face of the terrible suffering the world has known morally offensive. What on earth would "life after death" mean for those young children who died?

It is for those reasons that, while I have a considerable respect for Brian Hebblethwaite as a theologian and philosopher and indeed consider him a friend, I cannot follow his conclusions in his final chapter.

Anthony Thistleton

Thistleton has had a distinguished academic career as Professor of Theology at Nottingham University and then at Chester University and his main subject is hermeneutics, or the theory and methodology of interpreting tests, especially biblical texts. After a near fatal heart attack he resolved to write a major work on eschatology, published as *The Last Things: A New Approach.*[48]

He states in the Introduction that Chapter 2 "remains especially relevant to those who hold doubts about any kind of Christian hope in life after death. Such doubt is not limited to those outside the Church. Only exceptional Christians never experience even the faintest doubt about what lies beyond death. Our hope and confidence cannot be based on the capacities of human beings to survive death and to become immortal. Such confidence depends entirely on *God's promise* of resurrection and new creation. Everything depends here on *trust in God*, not on self-reliance."[49]

He examines what is meant by God's promise and asks "Can we be certain that the promises of God expressed in the Bible have the status of *divine* promises rather than human words of hope projected into the mouth of God?"[50] That is a good question, and Thistleton's answer appears to be that if people trust in those promises they prove to be effective in people's lives so they must be of God. Certainly it is possible to trust a promise in a way that makes that promise effective. To take a very different example, look at the effect of the false promise of a Hitler or a Stalin on hosts of people who believed them and went on to do terrible things. Surely the question to be asked about any promise is not simply whether it is effective, but whether it has the hallmarks of truthfulness. There is no escaping the personal judgment each person has to make about the validity of any promise whoever makes it, and ascribing views to God is a very uncertain business.

In the context of belief in life *after* death what has been said above shows there are significant differences between different Christians. What is somewhat surprising in Thiselton's book is that while he quotes some of those who take a divergent view from him (Barth quoted quite extensively, Rahner and Tillich less so), he nowhere examines the nature of their particular understanding of eternity. Neither does he examine the views of those who take a different view; Edwards, Hartshorne, Kung, Macquarrie and Pittenger are not even mentioned in the Index of Names.

However, in Chapter 8.3 he considered "Eternity as Timelessness, Everlasting Duration, Simultaneity, or Multidimensional and Transformed Reality." In the first, he notes that most theologians acknowledge that eternity suggests a complete termination of time. Of the second, where eternity involves temporal sequence and everlasting duration, while that appeals to Old Testament notions of "the living God" he notes "there are enormous difficulties in placing God among the temporal and contingent entities he has created. Augustine and Aquinas are surely right to accord to God a special status different in kind from the creatures he has created." His third view[51] he calls Simultaneity, based on Boethius. "Eternity is a mode of existence that is, on Boethius' view, neither reducible to time, nor incompatible with the reality of time. This facing both ways probably encounters least difficulties compared with the other two approaches, but suffers from some ambiguity and oversimplification."[52] That leads to his fourth approach "Multidimensional and Transformed Reality." He asserts that time is *not one thing.* He agrees with David Wilkinson that "God has both eternal and temporal poles to his nature....We need to see time as a fundamental part of eternity ... but we need the notion of multiple dimensions." He says his "close agreement with Wilkinson arises from the fact ... that the discussion founders because writers talk of 'time' rather than of *'our'* time, *social* time, *clock* time, and *God's* time as something quite different from each other."

All of that may or may not be true, although I note that many of the theologians I discussed earlier still thought that eternity is beyond time, and that human beings are nonetheless time bound creatures. I can only say that personally I can find nothing in Thistleton's argument to persuade me otherwise.

Dale C Allison

Dale Allison's book on the Last Things[53] was published in 2016. He says in the preface that it was not designed "to persuade through the arguments of an even-handed historian ... rather it was a personal theological exploration. It's an attempt to move from reconstructing the past to pondering the future."[54] He notes that many, including personal friends of his, doubt any form of an afterlife and he comments: "although I understand, I don't agree. I don't know how to be indifferent to the possibility of a world to come. For me, Christianity without hope beyond death is of reduced significance and of diminished interest."[55]

He notes that in America, belief in bodily resurrection is very limited and polls suggest belief in it is less popular than belief in immortality of the soul, reincarnation or even belief in extinction. Is, then, the alternative materialism? Allison says that while he is dubious about materialism he has nothing to offer in its place.

I am neither a dualist nor a pluralist nor a dual-aspect monist but rather, on this subject, an agnostic, intrigued by various possibilities, committed to none.... My only conviction is, despite all our scientific progress, matter remains a profound mystery, consciousness remains a profound mystery, and the self remains a profound mystery, so their relationship remains a profound mystery.... In the meantime, however, I don't feel compelled to cast my lot with the materialists.... The problem is this: If the strict materialists are right, I don't see how, once dead, we can ever live again.[56]

In a chapter on judgment he considers the "life reviews" that are part of Near-Death Experiences. "I wish to be clear. I am neither insisting that the life review is there because God put it there nor confidently equating the experience with divine judgment. My discussion is rather a way of fumbling toward some constructive analogy or useful parable. My goal is to find a helpful myth as opposed to an unhelpful myth." Interestingly, Macquarrie had a similar view of such life reviews which he saw as part of the process of changing our view of the past while still alive.[57] Allison also firmly rejects any notions of hell as permanent punishment and noted that even John Stott, a notable Anglican Evangelical, accepted the advice of the Church of England's Doctrine Commission in 1995 and construed hell as total non-being.[58]

In his final chapter, "Heaven and Experience," he considers three conceptions of the afterlife – heaven as angelic existence, heaven as reunion with family and friends, and heaven as an incomparably beautiful landscape. He certainly hopes for something like that, but his open-mindedness about what it might be is more attractive than the certainties of some others mentioned here, and his hopes remain that and not certainties.

However, he also noted the former Bishop of Stockholm Krister Stendahl in a Nobel Conference Lecture in1972, suggested that any personal concern for an afterlife was theologically suspect because it is self-centered: it privileges the individual over wider concerns. That is certainly part of my concern about those who are all too certain about life after death and I am not convinced by Allison's response when he says he wishes to distinguish between selfishness and a proper concern for the self. The two so easily elide.

What I find most surprising in his book is that he nowhere examines the view of eternity advanced by Wittgenstein and expressed by Barth, Rahner, Macquarrie, Hartshorne, Pittenger and Edwards, none of whom even feature in his index. There is an alternative to believing in life after death in any temporal sense, and it does mean recognizing that what is important in the long term is not our fate but God.

A Possible Conclusion

I find none of those alternative views convincing, either because they did not consider Wittgenstein's notion of eternity or because in Hebblethwaite's case, he advanced an alternative that I also found unconvincing for the reasons given. Let me end this chapter with someone with whom I do agree.

Hubert J. Richards was born in 1921 and was ordained as a Roman Catholic in 1946. His academic ability was recognized by his appointment as scripture professor at St Edmund's College, Ware and in 1965 he was appointed Principal of Corpus Christi College in London. While he started with a good relationship with Cardinal Heenan, it became more difficult as time went by, Richards being sympathetic to various developments in the Catholic Church that the far more conservative Heenan opposed. Richards retired as Principal of the College in 1972 and resigned as a Roman Catholic priest in 1975. He married a former nun and was invited to be a lecturer at Keswick Hall College in Norwich, an Anglican Teachers Training College. He remained in that post for many years and wrote a series of books, starting with *The Miracles of Jesus: What Really Happened?* And followed them with books on the First Christmas and the First Easter with the same strap line. Then in 1980 he wrote *Death and After: What Will Really Happen?*[59] All of the books were written for a popular audience without the sort of footnotes and quotations that my book has, but they were also very clearly academically well informed by his very wide reading. He died in 2010.[60]

In his book on death he quoted John Donne "Death be not Proud" and said:

> In other words, we have no need to fear death, because we won't really die or come to an end. The truth is, of course, that we will. To gloss over this fact is dishonest, and no less so for being thought the Christian thing to do. Human life does come to an end, and however painful the realization of this may be, we do psychological harm to ourselves by taking refuge behind talk of 'sleep' or 'release' or 'passing on'. There is a tragic finality about death, which we must take seriously or it is not death we are talking about. The Christian may wish to add further comments of his own, but unless what he has to say is based on the reality of death, it is building on a lie.[61]

I agree with that, as I suspect would some of the other theologians I have quoted in this chapter. That is partly because I believe the physical nature of human beings in undeniable. We come into existence through conception and death means the end of the physical body and hence the mind and brain and any personal self-consciousness. But I also believe in this life we can have intimations of things that are eternal in the sense that Wittgenstein suggested. I agree with the comment of Martin Rees in Chapter 5 that music is the language of religion and it certainly has the capacity to take us out of our immediate thoughts to help us reflect on emotions connected with what seem eternal and of ultimate value. Maybe art and meditation are other routes. So, I don't think our physical lives are the last word about us, which is why I don't find the views of those like Barth and Rahner in any way reductionist.

Richards suggests among other things that the memory of us will last at least for a period after our deaths, even if only in our families and perhaps especially our children, and those memories may continue to be influential on others. Certainly I can think of some who have died whose influence continues to affect how I think, including my parents but also respected teachers and valued friends. The continuation of our influence beyond death is not nothing, and whatever sort of mark we have made on the world becomes part of a wider consciousness. That does not just apply to those who have personally done anything significant; in their way even the memory of those children slaughtered in such horror by the Nazis in Auschwitz remains influential. The memory of the world to which every human being contributes becomes part of eternal life and therefore part of the memory of God, and I believe those children are held in the memory of God.

Richards commented on the corporate nature of this in his earlier book *The First Easter: What Really Happened.*

To speak of the resurrection of the body is to speak of the sharing by all men in the future of mankind and in the world we live in. The difficulty we have in coping with this idea stems from our western individualism. We are used to thinking in terms of 'my' soul, 'my' salvation, 'my' union with God. The biblical hope is not so self-centered. Salvation is to be bodily. And if the body is the way in which we are related to each other, then the final resurrection of the body cannot be said to have been achieved until all men are fully related to each other. We cannot speak of our own bodily resurrection without including the resurrection of all men, indeed of the whole universe. We cannot profess our faith in the resurrection of the body without hoping to be embodied in each other. And insofar as we already have some experience of this here and now, the resurrection of the body has begun, and in fact is going on all the time.[62]

He returned to the issue of individualism in his later book on *Death and After*.

In dying our relationship to God's creation takes on a new dimension. Instead of being safely insulated from the world around us, we enter into a deep communion with it. Instead of being isolated from our fellow human creatures, we are finally at one with them. Instead of being embodied in one human individual, we are now embodied in all.[63]

He acknowledges that some might see that as a loss of individuality, but he responds:

But what if individuality, far from being a prize possession that must be safeguarded at all costs, is in fact an obstacle to our real fulfillment? What if our human personality, far from being diminished by being embodied in the human community, is thereby perfected? For our true self does not consist – as it seems to do for things – in an individual separateness, but in an ability to communicate. Personality in fact cannot exist except in terms of relationship with others. If that relationship extends to all, the personality is enriched not impoverished.[64]

That, which is also implicit in what John Robinson and John Macquarrie wrote, I believe, is an essential. We have seen in this chapter the wide range of debates there has been since the middle of the last century within the church about the nature of life after death, or what I would prefer to call life *beyond* death.

Conclusion

In this chapter and indeed in this book as a whole I have come to some conclusions.

- First, the vast majority of philosophers and scientists, especially neuroscientists, believe human beings are psychosomatic unities and notions of an independent "soul" do not ultimately make any sense.
- Second, Wittgenstein's notion of eternity makes more sense than those suggested by some other theologians.
- Third, any talk of any individual life beyond death can only be seen as part of humanity's as a whole.
- Fourth, the Christian understanding of God is broad enough to encompass a range of views on eschatology.
- Fifth, whatever the Christian Church believes must be consistent with what we know about the world from other areas of knowledge as indicated, for example, in Chapters 4 and 5.

Those convictions inform my final summary chapter.

Chapter 6 Endnotes

1   Matthews WR. *The Hope of Immortality.* Epworth Press; 1966. p. 37.

2   Macquarrie J. *Christian Hope.* Mowbrays; 1978. p. 90.

3   Edwards DL. *After Death? Past Beliefs and Real Possibilities.* Cassell; 1999.p.71.

4   Swinburne R. *Are We Bodies or Souls?* OUP; 2019.

5   Swinburn. p. 1.

6   Ward K. *The Christian Idea of God.* CUP; 2017. p. 75.

7   Macquarrie. p. 113.

8   Rahner K. *Foundations of Christian Faith.* Translated by William V Dych. London: Darton Longman and Todd; 1978. Originally published in German in 1976. p. 434.

9   Rahner. p. 435f.

10 Wittengenstein L. *Tractatus Logico-philosophicus.* Thesis 6,4311. This was first published in German in 1921, but the sixth English edition was published London 1959.

11 Bultmann R. *History and Eschatology.* The Gifford Lectures 1955. Edinburgh: The University Press; 1957.

12 A google search for "Karl Barth and the afterlife" brings up the PostBarthian website, including an extensive if reworked summary of Barth's argument in Church Dogmatics, The Doctrine of Creation III. 2 Para 47.5 published in 1945.

13 Barth K. *Letters 1961–1968.* Eng Trans. Edinburgh: T.& T. Clark; 1981

14 Rahner. p. 436f.

15 Robinson J. *In the End God.* SCM Press; 1968. pp. 100–1.

16 Robinson J. *But That I Can't Believe.*Fontana: Collins; 1967. p. 45.

17 pp. 45–6.

18 Macquarrie J. *Principles of Christian Theology.* SCM Press; 1977. p. 360.

19 *PCT.* p.369.

20 *Christian Hope.* p.120.

21 Pittenger N. *After Death Life in God.* SCM Press; 1980. p. 4.

22 p. 58.

23 Edwards DL. *Asking Them Questions.* OUP; 1973. p. 56.

24 Pittenger. p. 58f.

25 Wiles M. *God's Action in the World. The Bampton Lectures for 1986.* London: SCM Press.

26 Proceedings of the British Academy Volume 161.

27 *The Christian Idea of God.* p. 12.

28 PCT. p. 104.

29 PCT. p. 88.

30 PCT. p. 116.

31 PCT. p. 118.

32 PCT. p. 120.

33 TCI of G. p. 46.

34 PCT. p. 75.

35 *Christian Hope.* p. 112.

36 *Christian Hope.* p. 120.

37 TCI of G. pp. 163–165.

38 PCN. pp. 147–148.

39 Polkinghorne J. *Belief in God in an Age of Science.* Yale University Press; 1998. p. 22

40 Edwards DL. *After Death? Past Beliefs and Real Possibilities.* Cassell; 1999. p.105.

41 David Edwards. p. 106.

42 Hick J. *Death and Eternal Life.* London: Collins; 1976.

43 Edwards. p. 105.

44 Hebblethwaite B. *The Christian Hope.* First published in 1984 by Marshall, Morgan and Scott. Revised Edition published in 2010 by OUP.

45 p. 199.

46 p. 205.

47 Greenberg I. "Cloud of Smoke, Pillar of Fire" Morgan M.

(ed). *A Holocaust Reader*. OUP; 2001. p. 107f.

48 Thistleton AC. *The Last Things: A New Approach*. SPCK; 2012.

49 p. xiii.

50 p. 45.

51 p. 141. His third view

52 p. 142.

53 Allison DC. *Night Comes: Death, Imagination and the Last Things*. Eerdmanns; 2016.

54 p. ix.

55 p. 16.

56 p. 37.

57 Macquarrie. *Christian Hope*. p. 119.

58 Allison. p. 100.

59 Richard HJ. *Death and After: What will Really Happen?* A Fount Original; 1980.

60 *A Voice Crying in the Wilderness: Hubert Richards: What really Happened* is a biography written by his wife, Clare Richards. Dublin: Columba Press; 2011.

61 *Death and After: What will Really Happen?* p. 24.

62 Richards HJ. *The First Easter: What Really Happened?* First published 1976 by Fontana Books, issued as a Fount paperback 1980. p. 95.

63 p. 99.

64 p. 99f.

Bibliography

In addition to all the books mentioned in the above Endnotes I should also add:

Vernon M. *A Secret History of Christianity: Jesus, the Last Inkling, and the Evolution of Consciousness*. Hampshire: John Hunt Publishing; 2019, especially Chapter 6, "Christ Consciousness" and pages122–133.

Chapter 7

A Personal Statement

I am at the moment perfectly healthy and well but I am writing this at the height of the COVID-19 crisis, and I know that at my age I am considered a vulnerable person who may well die if I catch it. Obviously I do not want that, so I strictly follow the Government advice about social distancing, and will certainly try to battle with the disease if I get it. But I am also aware than on April 3 2020 Angela Tilby, a regular columnist to the Church Times, wrote an article "Do we believe in life after death?" in the context of the Church of England dealing with the virus crisis. She wanted the church to say firmly that it believed in life after death, but she made a number of other points. "I suspect that if the C of E was to say anything about faith in the resurrection to eternal life at the moment, it would be angrily dismissed." "I can't help but be aware that in other times of mortal illness priests have administered the sacraments to the sick and dying and buried the dead, without regard for their own safety, even expecting to die as a result." She also said "I personally know many priests who do not believe in life after death, preferring to dwell on hope for a better world."

I certainly hope for a better world – who could not in the present circumstances? – but that is not *why* I do not believe in life *after* death. Tilby's comment diminishes much of what was said in the previous chapter. Rather, I believe in life *beyond* death, not in the sense of a temporal hope but in a conviction about the nature of eternity. Of course I share everyone's fear of death, although in my case it is more a fear of dying in very unpleasant circumstances, but I am a Christian because I believe the Christian faith conveys truth about eternal values. That certainly does not mean I believe every doctrinal statement the Christian Church has made over the two thousand years of its history – some of them were plain daft – we must be discriminating about our theological tradition. But there are eternal values worth stating, albeit briefly here.

First, I agree with Aquinas (and Macquarrie) that God is not *a* being among other beings in the universe (or even a multiverse), but is Being itself. I also agree with Macquarrie about his understanding of the relationship between belief in God and the scientific understandings of how the world is, however tentative and provisional those understandings might be. That is why I share his view that "human life seems to us so bound up with the human body that we cannot envisage for it any reality when the body is dissolved" and that "it is easier to see the possibility of cosmic hope and to embrace it than to entertain the hope for the individual beyond death." But I also believe that loving Being itself is the basis of a life worth living. I value immensely the opportunities life offers and am hugely grateful for them. Being grateful for being alive and therefore being grateful to God is a core part of my personal convictions.

Secondly, the example of Jesus Christ is one I reflect on daily. John Robinson's description of Jesus as the "Human Face of God" was a very good one; Jesus shows us what God is like in a way no one else does. That was partly by his teaching; "love God" and "love your neighbor" are good principles by which to live your life, but most of all it was by his example. His emphasis on the need to demonstrate forgiveness is another core part of my personal convictions. Of course that is sometimes difficult, especially to those who have done harm to those I care for or to me, but the statement attributed to Jesus in Luke's account of the passion "Father forgive them for they know not what they do" is never far from my mind. The crucifixion is a turning point in the history of the world for it demonstrates that God shares with us in this world's suffering. I agree with Bonheoffer, "only a suffering God can help." That suffering God is also, according to Jesus, a forgiving God.

But the crucifixion was not the end. As will have been evident from Chapter 3 of this book, I am not at all sure exactly what it was that led to the belief in the resurrection, but out of death on a cross came something transformational for the life of the world. The memory and example of Jesus Christ continues to make a difference to the way many live, including me, and in that sense He certainly lives on.

One consequence must include sacrificial living and Angela Tilby has a point about how priests served their communities in the past. However, context is everything and I also believe married clergy are valuable for those churches that have them. That means clergy carry obligations to their families as well as to their parishioners. If I die as a result of being irresponsible about maintaining social distance in the current virus crisis not only would I add to the demands on the NHS, but I would also cause a crisis for my wife and daughter. That does not remove the fact that a measure of self-sacrificial living is part of being a Christian, but it creates a context in which to reflect on self-sacrifice.

Thirdly, despite its alarming lack of critical theological thinking at present, I do value the Christian Church and especially the Church of England, which I have served in one form or another for over fifty years. I know that behind the appalling blandness of too many contemporary episcopal statements there are members of the church, both ordained and lay, who do think carefully and critically as the previous chapter has shown. If the church were more honest and self-critical than it is at the moment and if it seriously engaged with the doubts and questions of many who are on its fringe or who have even given up because of its unthinking blandness then I still believe it could be of significant service to the nation it seeks to serve. I remain a member of the Church of England, albeit a critical and often irritated member.

Fourthly, that serious engagement with the questions of our society should extend to what we think about death. Given the range of opinion among clergy that Angela Tilby partly recognizes, I wonder whether that ought to extend to the wording of the funeral service. I am aware of one clerical friend who is very reluctant to take a funeral service because of what he is expected to say in the liturgy about resurrection. In practice most funeral addresses dwell on the memory of the person who has died and the way those memories live on, so personally I can live with the funeral service with that in mind and interpret the language of resurrection as poetry. We all know that turning poetry into prose can involve a cheap dumbing down. But any knowledge of national statistics on what is believed about life after death as shown at the end of Chapter 4 shows that in almost any congregation at a funeral service there will be those who find some of the language hard to accept. If the church is really to seek to serve the nation it should reflect on that fact, and as the previous chapter shows, it needs to reflect on its own theological tradition as well. There has to be some meeting point that bridges the divide between religious language and a rational, scientific view of what happens when we die. Some of the theologians quoted in the previous chapter provided that.

Of course, none of us knows exactly what we shall think when death approaches, but when that happens to me, I suspect thinking I would live on with personal consciousness in some mysterious way afterwards would not help. Death is the end of life. In many ways I have had a good life so have plenty of reasons to be thankful, although I realize that in the whole history of the world that is certainly not what many people who died in far grimmer circumstances thought.

But hope for the future at that point should not be about me, but about God. Part of what Paul described as being "in Christ" means that anyone who is a follower of Jesus Christ shares in however a minor way in that tradition. That is why I agree with the Richards' quotation towards the end of the previous chapter about the consequences of western individualism; we do not contribute to the life of the world simply by ourselves, but we do so as part of a wider community. Richards wrote that "We cannot speak of our own bodily resurrection without including the resurrection of all men, indeed of the whole universe." Macquarrie wrote "the past that is perished for us is still present in God." I suspect that is related to what Norman Pittenger said about being in the memory of God. It is in that combination of Richards', Macquarrie's and Pittenger's views that I find my hope. But it is hope in God, who incorporates the memories of us, and therefore the contribution each person has made towards what God intended us to be, that continues. Ultimately it is the corporate, not the individual that counts.

I therefore personally share Dag Hammarskjold's view "For all that has been, Thanks! To all that shall be, Yes!" But I do not see any individualistic conscious life *after* death as part of what shall be.

Postscript

Facing Dying

This book so far has mainly been about the notion of life after death. But there are also debates about the actual process of dying, not least within the Church of England. For that reason, I include this postscript.

Each year about half a million people die in England, two-thirds of them over 75 years of age. Managing the process of dying has received considerable attention in this century, but in recent years three factors have made it more complicated.

First, advances in medical science mean that death can be delayed for a much longer period than might have been the case earlier and so a terminal illness can last far longer, sometimes to the distress of the patients and their families.

Secondly, the conviction in 2000 of Harold Shipman, a medical practitioner in Hyde in Manchester, on fifteen counts of the murder of elderly patients led to the subsequent Shipman Inquiry, which reported that he had probably been responsible for the deaths of nearly 250 people by giving a drug normally used for pain control in cancer cases. He never admitted his crimes, and in 2004 committed suicide in prison. The inquiry led to some changes in certifying deaths and in dispensing practices, which some believe has led to a reluctance to over-prescribe pain relieving drugs even to the extent in some cases of under prescribing them. It is at least arguable that for a period it also damaged public confidence in the medical profession.

Thirdly, there is a more general willingness on the part of many members of the public to question the advice of specialists, including medical specialists. These factors put doctors in a far more difficult position when dealing with the dying, especially when family members of the patient disagree with one another about any withdrawal of treatment.

In 2008 the Department of Health published its End of Life Care Strategy. Its Executive Summary identified four factors most people consider constitutes a "good death," being treated as an individual with dignity and respect, being without pain and other symptoms, being in familiar surroundings, being in the company of close family and friends. However, they also noted "Some people do die as they would have wished, but many others do not. Some people experience excellent care in hospitals, hospices, care homes and in their own homes. But the reality is many do not. Many people experience unnecessary pain and other symptoms. There are distressing reports of people not being treated with dignity and respect and many people do not die where they would choose to."

As part of Care Planning they wrote "All people approaching the end of life need to have their needs assessed, their wishes and preferences discussed and an agreed set of actions reflecting the choices they make about their care recorded in a care plan. In some cases, people may want to make an advance decision to refuse treatment, should they lack capacity to make such a decision in the future. Others may want to set out more general wishes and preferences about how they are cared for and where they would wish to die. These should all be incorporated in a care plan."

One method of dealing with this was known as the Liverpool Care Pathway (LCP), which had been developed in the 1990s in the Royal Liverpool University Hospital in conjunction with the Marie Curie Palliative Care Institute. Its purpose was to provide the best possible care for those dying in the last days and hours of their lives and was widely seen as a way of transferring the "excellence" of the best hospice care to hospitals and care homes. However, over the years critical comments were made about it and the Department of Health set up an independent review panel in 2013 under the chairmanship of Baroness Neuberger.

The review, "More Care, Less Pathway," noted that some

good things had been achieved and that when the scheme was operated by well trained, well-resourced and sensitive teams it had worked well, with relatives of people who had died under it feeling their loved ones had a good death. But there was also much criticism of the process by some patients' families. Three factors particularly attracted critical comments. First, some patients' families were not consulted even though the original report said they should be. Secondly, criticism arose because financial incentives that had been offered to institutions that put patients on the care pathway were sometimes regarded, probably wrongly, as a financial incentive to hasten someone's death. Thirdly, in some cases hydration and nutrition were denied to patients. This might be justified if not doing so would cause patients distress, but, as the review put it, "refusing food and drink is a decision for the patient, not for the clinical staff to make."

"More Care, Less Pathway" recommended the LCP scheme be abandoned by the Department of Heath and it was replaced by individual care plans devised for each patient. How well that works will vary and of course the NHS is always under great pressure. With the continuing difficulties of getting agreement among patients and their families about what they want, and sometimes even disagreement between medical staff on what the best way forward should be, this potentially puts medical staff responsible for the medical decisions about individual patients in an invidious position.

A fundamental question in facing death is whether the patient wants death to be avoided for as long as possible or is content to embrace it when the time comes. Medical staff also have different views on that. Within my own family I have had experience of the issue. Shortly after I was ordained I accompanied my mother to see her elderly and much loved aunt who, well into her 80s, had been taken ill. When we saw her in hospital, she appeared content and said she was "ready to go." When a doctor came and gave her an injection of antibiotics my mother asked whether that was really for the best, and was treated as though she was simply a grasping relative anxious for her aunt's money, which was very far from the truth. The consequences of the doctor's action meant an old lady had another six months of pretty unbearable mental suffering before she finally died. The Hippocratic Oath is sometimes summarized as "Do no harm"; at the time both my mother and I thought prolonging her life in that way did harm. When my mother was dying some years later I knew very clearly what her wishes were and the doctor responsible for her care accepted that. She was made comfortable and given basic palliative care, but the hospital did not "strive officiously to keep alive." Both my brother and I were grateful, as we knew that was what she had wanted.

One practical step individuals can take is to make a "living will" or advanced care plan well before they die. According to a 2012 British Attitudes Survey 70% of the population feel comfortable in talking about death, while 13% do not, but that does not translate into action about living wills. The survey found only 5% of the population has made one as opposed to 11% who have made wills. Where someone's wishes are clearly stated then, if relatives have a copy, that will give some clear guidance to doctors. Of course an individual may well want to be kept alive as long as possible, and if that is their wish I am sure it should be respected, but it is legally possible to identify the circumstances in which a patient might not wish their life to be artificially prolonged, but be permitted to die naturally. They can ask that they only receive treatment that will alleviate pain or distressing symptoms so as to make them comfortable, even if that has the effect of shortening life. Administering drugs for the specific purpose of relieving pain, which may nonetheless have the side effect of shortening life, is not illegal. The whole matter might be described as a gray area although, of course, it certainly falls short of euthanasia. Personally, I have made a living will.

Euthanasia remains illegal in the United Kingdom, but that does not mean it has never been practiced. The most notable example was the death of King George V in 1936, although the details only became public fifty years later. Lord Dawson, the Royal Physician, was caring for the King whose health had not been good for many years; he had suffered from pulmonary disease, pleurisy and, later, septicemia. In his final year he was occasionally administered oxygen. Early on the evening of January 20 1936, by which time the King was unconscious, Lord Dawson wrote a brief medical bulletin that declared "The King's life is moving peacefully towards its close." Later the Archbishop of Canterbury, Cosmo Lang, came to say prayers at the King's bedside and then left. Dawson then administered morphine and cocaine and within an hour the King was dead. Dawson's notes said that Queen Mary and the Prince of Wales had told him that they did not want the King's life needlessly prolonged if his illness was clearly fatal, but it is not known how explicit Dawson was with them about what he did. According to his notes he did it because "the last stage might endure for many hours, unknown to the patient but little comporting with the dignity and the serenity which he so richly merited and which demanded a brief final scene." More controversially he also wrote that this meant the announcement could be carried "in the morning papers rather than the less appropriate evening journals."

A few months after the King's death Dawson spoke in the House of Lords against a bill that would have legalized euthanasia, but he opposed it because he believed the matter was best left to individual physicians rather than to official regulators. "One should make the act of dying more gentle and more peaceful even if it does involve the curtailment of the length of life. That has increasingly become the custom. This may be taken as something accepted." The Archbishop of Canterbury,

Cosmo Lang, spoke after Dawson's speech and praised it.

The more detailed knowledge of what had happened medically in the case of George V's death only emerged to the public 50 years later and thirty-six years after Dawson himself had died. It was reported by Dawson's biographer who had not included it in his original biography at the request of Dawson's widow, but it was published in a magazine "History Today" and in the New York Times in 1986. Some were appalled, including Kenneth Rose the biographer of George V, who said "In my opinion the King was murdered by Dawson." Others might take a more sympathetic approach to leaving such matters to trusted medical advisers.

Deliberate euthanasia nonetheless remains illegal. If any doctor today followed Dawson's example, and it became publicly known, he or she might well face a public trial. Any doctor caring for those who are dying will be aware that others, medical staff and families, might well be watching carefully what the doctor does and might report him or her. For that reason there is reluctance among some doctors to take actions that they might otherwise consider to be in the best interests of their patients because of an understandable professional concern about being reported and even prosecuted.

However, there remain a number of people in the United Kingdom who wish to take control of when, where and how they die. There have been some high profile court cases where individuals have asked the Courts to allow them to seek assisted dying, but the Courts have always taken the view that any change in the law requires a decision by Parliament. Against that background it is not surprising that some choose to take advantage of opportunities of dying in other countries, most notably the Dignitas Clinic in Switzerland, a country where assisted dying is permitted.

Assisting someone to commit suicide is illegal in the UK, potentially punishable by 14 years in prison. Following the case of Debbie Purdy, which received a lot of press attention at the time, in 2010 the then Director of Public Prosecutions, Sir Keir Starmer, produced guidelines that indicated the circumstances in which his office would be inclined to initiate or not to initiate prosecution. In general if the patient "had reached a voluntary, clear, settled and informed decision to commit suicide," if the person who helped them had first tried to persuade them not to do so, was wholly motivated by compassion and had sought to discourage the patient from taking the action, those would be factors that might lead to them not being prosecuted. The 2010 guidelines did say that no medical staff could be involved in providing such assistance, so it would always be essentially amateur help, although that was subsequently modified by Starmer's successor so that only those who had the direct medical responsibility for the patient were excluded. Many considered the provision of guidelines a helpful move, although inevitably others were critical. Managing dying is always a potentially controversial matter.

As of March 2018 euthanasia, when a doctor takes specific action to end someone's life, is legal in the Netherlands, Belgium, Luxembourg, Columbia, and Canada. Assisted suicide, where patients have to take the final act themselves, is legal in those countries, in Switzerland and in the US States of Washington, Oregon, Colorado, Hawaii, Vermont and California and in Washington DC. An assisted dying scheme in the Australian state of Victoria came into effect in mid-2019, and that was followed by Western Australia doing something similar.

This means there is experience to learn from elsewhere. In Oregon the law was changed as a result of a citizen's initiative passed twice by Oregon voters in 1994 but implementation was delayed until October 1997 when the Act came into force. A measure to repeal it was put on the general election ballot in November of that year, and voters chose to retain the Act by a margin of 60% to 40%. There is therefore over 20 years of experience in that state to learn from. A significant difference is that in the UK the National Health Service provides medical care free at the point of delivery, while all medical care in Oregon has to be covered by insurance, and there are some diseases where insurance cover is very expensive. That does make it a different context, but otherwise the Oregon experience has been influential in considering the matter both in other States in America and here.

The possibility of assisted suicide in this country has been widely debated in this century and opinion polls suggest that a majority would favor a change. In 2015 Populus, the Public Opinion Polling Organization carried out a survey, which included a number of questions relating to assisted dying. On the principle of allowing assisted dying in this country 82% supported it, with nearly half strongly supporting it and just over a third somewhat supporting it and 12% opposing it, equally divided between those who somewhat opposed it and those who strongly opposed it.

That substantial support for the principle might not be quite as firm as some have suggested, as there is evidence some individuals change their minds as a result of hearing arguments against a change in the law, particularly those who are concerned about family pressures on the elderly to agree to something that they might not personally really wish. But overall it does seem that a majority of the population is in favor of a change in the law.

Britain is a parliamentary democracy where issues of major moral importance are often decided by a free vote in both Houses of Parliament. Members will obviously be aware of public opinion, but are under no obligation to follow it; it is for individual members of each house to vote according to their consciences. The presence of two houses, one elected and one appointed, has its advantages because while members of the House of Commons will be aware of public opinion and particularly of their own constituents, the House of Lords contains members who are there not because of their particular political views but because of their often wide-ranging experience of complex moral issues, medical members of the House of Lords being a good example. The convention that ultimately the votes of the House of Commons are definitive is a wise way of maintaining proper democratic control.

In 1964 Parliament voted to end capital punishment with two third's majorities in both the House of Commons and the House of Lords, although public opinion at the time still showed a majority of the population in favor of its retention. From time to time, particularly following some especially dreadful murder, there have been calls for its reintroduction and a television poll in 2009 showed that 70% of the population still favored its re-introduction in certain circumstances, but in 2015 a poll showed that less than half of the population (48%) then did so. The fact that public opinion can be so volatile shows the reason why a proper, thorough debate by both Houses of Parliament weighing up the different moral arguments remains a sensible way for a mature democracy dealing with such complex issues. Public opinion polls are important evidence of what the majority of the population believe and that evidence should be clearly recognized in parliamentary debates, but that does not mean it should be slavishly followed.

The debate about assisted dying came to a head in Parliamentary debates, the most decisive one being in the House of Commons in 2015 where the proposal was to allow assisted dying for those whom two doctors confirmed had less than six months to live. Prior to those debates there had been much discussion, which continues today, in both secular and ecclesiastical circles.

Opposition to changes to the law to allow assisted dying has come from a number of sources. The Church of England Bishops in the House of Lords, disabled charities and some medical groups opposed the change, although the BMA had never allowed a formal poll of its doctors. Interestingly in February 2018 the editor of the *British Medical Journal* suggested that the BMA should now allow a formal poll. Whether that suggestion is accepted remains to be seen.

The opposition to any change in the law had a number of grounds.

1. They were concerned about vulnerable elderly people being pressurized by younger members of their families to take decisions to end their lives for what might have included financial reasons.

2. There was the fear of what was described as "a slippery slope"; that a decision to allow assisted dying in the case of those who faced a terminal illness and were likely to die within six months (as was the case in the bill before Parliament) would quickly be followed by pressure to allow it in other cases finally leading to a more general endorsement of euthanasia even in the case of those who were not able to make any informed decision for themselves. Understandably that was a particular concern of some of the groups campaigning on behalf of a particular disability, but the concern was certainly not confined to those groups.

3. Allowing Parliament to make it legal to take someone's life would be, as the present Archbishops described it, "crossing the Rubicon." Since the ending of capital punishment taking someone's life in this country can result in charges of murder or manslaughter being brought. Of course exceptional grounds might be the basis of a final not guilty decision – self-defense for example – but to end that prohibition on the taking of life would be a major change in the law.

4. Such a change would affect the relationship between

doctors and patients. At the moment patients could rely on the fact that the medical ethics of clinical practice was to seek to improve patients' quality of life, not to end them.

5. That good quality palliative care can normally alleviate distressing symptoms.

6. That only a minority of people wanted to end their lives, and the rules for the majority should not be changed to accommodate the wishes of a small group.

7. That being sure that any individual was likely to die within six months is very difficult, even though for the doctors making that decision the balance of probability was the criteria to be applied.

Those are all serious matters and deserve to be considered very carefully. But against those arguments is the fact that, while palliative care can certainly help many people, there are others for whom it does not work. Their distress is such that they would prefer to end their lives. Because some are financially and even physically not able to go to Dignitas in Switzerland and are physically unable to commit suicide without help which might well lead to others being prosecuted, their legal case is often that they are being denied their human right to commit suicide. Understandably the Courts have been cautious and unable to grant that without a change in the law authorized by Parliament.

In the Parliamentary debates in the House of Lords in 2014 and the House of Commons in 2015 one important amendment was introduced in the Committee stage of the House of Lords. It was agreed that in every case a High Court judge of the family division should be satisfied that the person "has a voluntary, clear, settled and informed wish to end his or her life." This meant that each case would be subject to a legal judgment on that central question. When the bill was debated later in the House of Commons Sir Keir Starmer, who as DPP had proposed the original guidelines for deciding whether a prosecution should be brought of someone assisting a suicide, said the reason in those guidelines he had not originally allowed a medical person to be involved was because there was no such legal mechanism available then. With this amendment that situation would be changed so it would be possible for competent medical assistance to be provided.

I believe the provision of that review in each case by the High Court was an adequate response to items 1 and 4 in the grounds for objections. It was also pointed out in the House of Commons debate that regarding item 2 the law could not be further changed without it coming back to Parliament, so any "slippery slope" would remain firmly in the hands of Parliament. Regarding item 3 the bill would certainly "cross the Rubicon," but it would only cross it in a case when the patient concerned clearly wanted it and that was confirmed by a High Court judge.

The 2015 debate in the House of Commons ended with the proposal being defeated by a two-thirds majority. Of course that did not end the debate and it continues still, with the House of Lords having a further discussion of the matter in 2017 and no doubt more cases will be brought before the courts. It may be some time before Parliament formally considers the issue again, but it is almost bound to happen at some stage. However, one of the concerns about the public debate is that, perhaps inevitably, the conversation becomes fractious and evidence is disputed.

One of the more difficult aspects is that good palliative care is sometimes presented as being in competition with assisted suicide. American States are subject to assessment for the quality of their palliative care and are listed in four categories. It is interesting that Oregon is assessed as being in the top quartile of States in the provision of Palliative Care, and the Board of Directors of the Oregon Hospice & Palliative Care Associations said in April 2017 that the Association "supports the rights of Oregonians to choose or not to choose any and all legal end-of-life options, and supports hospice and palliative care programs in development of their policies around the Oregon Death with Dignity Act and Physician-Assisted death." It is on the basis of the Oregon experience that other States in America have adopted very similar programs, and one of the arguments advanced in Oregon is that many are relieved to know that assisted suicide remains an option even though they do not take it.

In 2017 the Christian think-tank Theos published a book by Andrew Grey entitled *Dignity at the End of Life: What's Beneath the Assisted Dying Debate?* It examines the concept of dignity, as one that is often mentioned in the discussion about end of life care, and suggests that dignity is something that is shown to dying people rather than simply a demand for dignity in the autonomy of the patient. Certainly dignity has a wider application than simply a demand by any potential patient, but personally my reason for being sympathetic to those who want assisted dying is not so much on the grounds of dignity than on the grounds of simple compassion, which is a Christian quality. I recognize compassion is not confined to one side in this debate; it is compassion for the vulnerable that motivates, for example, the majority episcopal outlook. But Grey acknowledges that there are some for whom palliative care is not effective. When someone is in great pain and is finding their life so miserable that they want to die, insisting on prolonging their life seems to me to be cruel. I fully accept this is one of the great individual moral dilemmas of our time, and there are arguments on both sides of the debate.

Personally, I agreed with retired Archbishop George Carey when he changed his mind about assisted dying. Impressively he went to visit one of the patients who was requesting it and he wrote "It was the case of Tony Nicklinson that exerted the deepest influence on me. Here was a dignified man making a simple appeal for mercy, begging that the law allow him to die in peace, supported by his family. His distress made me question my motives in previous debates. Had I been putting doctrine before compassion, dogma before human dignity? I began to reconsider how to interpret Christian theology on the subject. As I did so, I grew less and less certain of my opposition to the right to die."

I do not normally agree with Archbishop Carey, but on this particular matter I believe he is right. That is why, although it is a huge dilemma, I am, just, on the side of changing the law and permitting assisted dying.

Index of Names and Topics

Acts of the Apostles 53f
Adrian, Edgar 116
Alcock, James 123
Alexander the Great 91,
Allen, Woody 93
Allison, Dale C 57, 69-75, 77f,
  156-158, 165
Almond, Philip 31f, 39, 45, 47,
  93-99, 110
apparitions of deceased
  people 71-74, 106
Aristotle 14-16, 29
Arjuna 22
Augustine St. 8,16, 33-37,
Augustine, Keith 100-107, 110
Badham, Paul 114
Baker, John Austin 57, 77
Barth, Karl 56f, 136f, 151, 158,
  160
Baumeister, Roy 94
Bennett, M. R. 115-119, 125,
  127, 130f, 135
Bentley Hart, David 126, 131,
  134
Bhagavad Gita 22,
Blackmore, Susan 120-124,
  130f
Blakemore, Colin 116, 130
Bowker, John 19,22, 30
Bonheoffer 39, 167
Brahman 22

brain 91, 101, 103, 121-129
Buddha (Gautama) 24-28, 118
Buddhism 24-28, 84
Bultmann, R 136, 163
Butler, R A 49

Calvin, John 42-43, 47
Camus, Albert 92, 110

cannibalism 36, 89f
capital punishment 179
Carey, George 183f
Carnley, Peter 57, 77
Cartesian dualism 44f, 79-82,
  87, 116f, 119-122, 128, 133f
Cartesian theatre 123
Cave, Stephen 89-95, 108, 110
Cebes 15, 85
Church of England 2, 77, 168,
  171, 179
ComRes Survey of belief in
  the Resurrection 75f, 107
consciousness 5-6, 92, 101f,
  122-129, 157
Copernicus, Nicolaus 128, 133
COVID-19 166
Crick, Francis 116, 130
Crossan, John Dominic 57-63,
  77
Crossley, James 65f, 77
Cryonics 6

Daniel 7f,

Dante, Alighieri 40-42, 91

Darwin, Charles 45, 128

dating of the New Testament 31, 48-54

Dawkins, Richard 100

Dawson, Lord 175

death, clinical definition of 114

Dennett, Daniel 123

Descartes, René 43-46, 47, 79

Dignitas Clinic 176

Dingwall, Eric 86, 109

double-predestination 43

Dunn, James 64f, 68f

Eccles, John 116

Ecclesiastes 7,

Edwards, David 133, 141f, 148-150, 151, 158

Einstein, Albert 92

Elijah 7

Empty Tomb 51, 57, 59f, 63, 74

End of Life Care Strategy 172

Enlightenment 9, 67f, 76,

Enoch 7

Epicurus 15, 85, 93

eschatology 17, 31, 42, 133, 136, 162

eternity 135, 137f, 151, 162, 166

euthanasia and assisted suicide 175, 177

evolution 45, 128

Fenton, John 66

Fenwick, Peter 114, 130

forgiveness 167

Freeman, Rabbi Helen 11, 29

funeral services 169

Galileo 5, 67, 128

Gallop, David 13

George V, death of 175

Goodman, Lenn E 20f, 30

Gospel of Peter (The Cross Gospel) 60-62

gratitude, 93f,

Greenberg, I153f , 164

Grey, Anthony i83

Greyson Scale 113

Hacker, P. M. S. 115-119, 125, 127, 130f, 135

Hammarskojld, Dag 170

Hariri, Yuval Noah 6, 29

Haywood, Rosalind 83, 86f

heaven 17, 23, 96, 104f, 157

Hebblethwaite, Brian 32f, 40, 41f, 43, 47, 138, 150-154, 158, 164

heliocentrism 128

hell 7f, 23, 32, 39-41, 62, 96f, 105, 132, 157

Hick, John 149f, 164

Hinduism 21-24

Holocaust 10, 153

House of Commons Debate 2015 182

House of Lords debate 2014 181
Husan, Usama 17, 30
Hussain AA 29

immortality 6, 89-95, 101, 139f, 141, 156
individualism 140, 160
Islam 16-21
Islamic humanism 20f

Jesus Christ 17, 48-75, 118, 121, 168
Jesus Seminar 58
John's Gospel 54-56
Judaism 6-11
judgment 18-21

karma 26, 105
Kenny, Anthony 11, 13, 29, 37, 45f, 47, 76, 80-82,107,109, 134
Kerr, Fergus 37f, 47
Khaldun. Ibn 21
Khayyam, Omar 19-20, 30
Koestler, Arthur 83, 87-89, 109
Krishna 22f
Kung, Hans 57, 77, 153

Lampe, Geoffrey 57, 153
Lang, Cosmo 175
LeDoux, J 117f, 130
Libet Test 124f
Life Review 112f, 141, 157
Limbo 18, 40, 41

Liverpool Care Pathway 172
Living Wills 174
Luke's Gospel 51-53, 56
Luther, Martin 42

Maccabean Revolt 8, 153
Macquarrie, John 133-135, 140-147, 149, 151-153, 157, 158, 161, 163, 165, 167, 170
Maimonides 9,15
Mark's Gospel 51f, 62
Marsh, Henry 126f, 131
Martin, Michael 104,110
Matthews, W R 132f, 163
Matthew's Gospel 51f, 56
Memory 5, 117f, 119, 127f, 141f, 160, 168
Mereological fallacy 117
mind 44, 79-82, 91, 102
Moody, Raymond 112
Moses 7
Muhammed 16, 21

Neo-Platonism 33,
near-death experiences 108, 112-129, 158
Neuberger, Baroness 172
neuroscience 45, 101-102, 115-129, 133, 162
New Scientist 86f
Nicklinson, Tony 183
Nirvana 22, 24, 26f

O'Brien, Barbara 30

Oregan Law 177

Origen 32f, 47

Paranormal 106

Parnia, Sam 112-115, 121f, 130f

Paul St 50, 169

Palliative Care 174, 182

Passingham, Richard, 124-126, 131

Penfold, Wilder 88

Pharisees 9

Pittenger, N 141f, 158, 164, 170

Plato 11-14, 34, 112

Platonism 8

Polkinghorne, John 148, 164

Populus Survey on Assisted Dying 178

psychosomatic unity 119, 133, 135, 162

Purgatory 44,97

Pythagoras 11

Qur'an 16-20

Rahner, Karl 96, 134f, 137, 151, 153, 158, 160, 163

reductionism 118f, 160

Rees, Dewi 72,

Rees, Martin 38f, 47, 118, 130, 159

Reimarus, Hermann 57

reincarnation 6, 23, 28f, 30

resurrection 6, 36f, 138f , 156, 169

Resurrection of Jesus 46, 48-76

Richards, H J 79, 158 – 161, 165, 170

Robertson J 67

Robinson, John A T 48, 138-140, 153, 161, 163, 167

Rose, Kenneth 180

Russell, Bertrand 88

Ryle, Gilbert 79-83, 109, 133

Sadducees 8

Sartori, Penny 114, 120

Savile, Jimmy 5

Schrodinger 88

Schweitzer, Albert 57

Second Temple Judaism 63, 66f

Seleucid Empire 8-9

self-sacrifice 168

Sellars, Wilfred 119, 153

Seneca 15f, 29

Sherrington, Charles 88, 116

Shipman Inquiry 171

Simon, Ulrich 83f

Society for Psychical Research 72, 86

Socrates 11 – 15, 85

Solomon, Rabbi Mark 9f, 29, 153

soul 6,12-15, 17, 23, 27, 34-36, 81f, 91, 101, 103, 115, 129, 134, 162

Southwark Cathedral 48,

Starmer, Sir Keir 177, 181

Stewart-Williams, Steve 99-101

Swinburne, R 126, 133f, 135, 163

Temple in Jerusalem 8, 9, 63f

Temple, Frederick 45, 128, 131

Temple, William 57,

theodicy 151

Thistleton, AC 154-156, 165

Thomas Aquinas 19, 33, 37-40, 92

Thomas, St (doubting Thomas) 55, 66

Tilby, Angela 166, 168

Toynbee, Arnold 83-87, 109

Tsuji, Takash 27

Vermes, Geza 9, 29

Von Glasenapp 25

Vernon, Mark 165

Ward, Keith 126, 134f, 142f, 163

West, T G 29

Wiles, Maurice 142, 153, 164

Wisdom literature 8, 93, 95, 108

Wittgenstein, Ludwig 46, 80f, 83, 107, 133, 136f, 151, 158, 159, 162, 163

Wright, N T 57, 63-70, 77f

Xenophon 11

Zionism 10

THE NEW OPEN SPACES

Throughout the two thousand years of Christian tradition there have been, and still are, groups and individuals that exist in the margins and upon the edge of faith. But in Christianity's contrapuntal history it has often been these outcasts and pioneers that have forged contemporary orthodoxy out of former radicalism as belief evolves to engage with and encompass the ever-changing social and scientific realities. Real faith lies not in the comfortable certainties of the Orthodox, but somewhere in a half-glimpsed hinterland on the dirt track to Emmaus, where the Death of God meets the Resurrection, where the supernatural Christ meets the historical Jesus, and where the revolution liberates both the oppressed and the oppressors.
Welcome to Christian Alternative... a space at the edge where the light shines through.
If you have enjoyed this book, why not tell other readers by posting a review on your preferred book site.
Recent bestsellers from Christian Alternative are:

Bread Not Stones
The Autobiography of An Eventful Life
Una Kroll
The spiritual autobiography of a truly remarkable woman and a history of the struggle for ordination in the Church of England.
Paperback: 978-1-78279-804-0 ebook: 978-1-78279-805-7

The Quaker Way
A Rediscovery
Rex Ambler
Although fairly well known, Quakerism is not well understood.
The purpose of this book is to explain how Quakerism works as
a spiritual practice.
Paperback: 978-1-78099-657-8 ebook: 978-1-78099-658-5

Blue Sky God
The Evolution of Science and Christianity
Don MacGregor
Quantum consciousness, morphic fields and blue-sky
thinking about God and Jesus the Christ.
Paperback: 978-1-84694-937-1 ebook: 978-1-84694-938-8

Celtic Wheel of the Year
Tess Ward
An original and inspiring selection of prayers combining
Christian and Celtic Pagan traditions, and interweaving their
calendars into a single pattern of prayer for every morning
and night of the year.
Paperback: 978-1-90504-795-6

Christian Atheist
Belonging without Believing
Brian Mountford
Christian Atheists don't believe in God but miss him: especially
the transcendent beauty of his music, language, ethics, and
community.
Paperback: 978-1-84694-439-0 ebook: 978-1-84694-929-6

Compassion Or Apocalypse?
A Comprehensible Guide to the Thoughts of René Girard
James Warren
How René Girard changes the way we think about God and the
Bible, and its relevance for our apocalypse-threatened world.
Paperback: 978-1-78279-073-0 ebook: 978-1-78279-072-3

Diary Of A Gay Priest
The Tightrope Walker
Rev. Dr. Malcolm Johnson
Full of anecdotes and amusing stories, but the Church is still a
dangerous place for a gay priest.
Paperback: 978-1-78279-002-0 ebook: 978-1-78099-999-9

Do You Need God?
Exploring Different Paths to Spirituality Even For Atheists
Rory J.Q. Barnes
An unbiased guide to the building blocks of spiritual belief.
Paperback: 978-1-78279-380-9 ebook: 978-1-78279-379-3

Readers of ebooks can buy or view any of these bestsellers by
clicking on the live link in the title. Most titles are published
in paperback and as an ebook. Paperbacks are available in
traditional bookshops. Both print and ebook formats are
available online.

Find more titles and sign up to our readers' newsletter at
http://www.johnhuntpublishing.com/christianity
Follow us on Facebook at
https://www.facebook.com/ChristianAlternative